Edward Everett Hayden

The Great Storm off the Atlantic Coast of the United States

March 11-14, 1888

Edward Everett Hayden

The Great Storm off the Atlantic Coast of the United States
March 11-14, 1888

ISBN/EAN: 9783337187002

Printed in Europe, USA, Canada, Australia, Japan

Cover: Foto ©ninafisch / pixelio.de

More available books at **www.hansebooks.com**

G. L. DYER, LIEUTENANT, U. S. N.,
Hydrographer to the Bureau of Navigation.

THE GREAT STORM

OFF THE

ATLANTIC COAST OF THE UNITED STATES

MARCH 11–14, 1888.

BY

EVERETT HAYDEN,
IN CHARGE OF THE DIVISION OF MARINE METEOROLOGY.

WASHINGTON:
GOVERNMENT PRINTING OFFICE.
1888.

3546 ST

PREFACE.

The accompanying monograph gives a brief but concise account of one of the most notable storms of this century. In its preparation the primary object has been to preserve the principal facts in a clear and intelligible form for such deductions as can be drawn from them hereafter. The work was commenced under the supervision of Commander J. R. Bartlett, U. S. Navy, who saw the importance of publishing, whenever possible, all data relative to marine meteorology in order to make them accessible to meteorologists for study and to contributing navigators, who naturally look for some return for their observations and reports. With this object in view, efforts have been made to put the Division of Marine Meteorology upon a footing commensurate with the importance of the subject, and at the same time to insure a certain amount of continuity in the services of its personnel, without which the successful prosecution of the study of the subject is impossible. The support of Commodore John G. Walker, U. S. Navy, chief of Bureau of Navigation, who has cordially approved of every effort to increase the efficiency and usefulness of the Hydrographic Office, both to the naval service and to the merchant marine, has rendered it possible to carry these plans into effect, although the field covered is so vast that long continued and persistent effort will be necessary to secure a really effective organization. It will, therefore, be understood that this account has been prepared under certain difficulties which have delayed its publication, but which, it is hoped, will not diminish its value. Mr. Everett Hayden, U. S. Navy, the author of this monograph, as chief of the Division of Marine Meteorology, is the editor of the Pilot Chart of the North Atlantic Ocean. In addition to the regular four years' course of study at the U. S. Naval Academy and three years' experience at sea, he has had a tour of duty at the Smithsonian Institution, Washington, and has served with the U. S. Geological Survey and at the observatory of Harvard University. His assistants have been Ensign Ernest Wilkinson, U. S. Navy, and Messrs. O'Leary, Lerch, and Dutton, all graduates of the Naval Academy.

GEORGE L. DYER,
Lieutenant, U. S. Navy, Hydrographer.

WEATHER CHART.--MARCH 11.

Meteorological conditions at noon, Greenwich mean time (7 A. M., 75th meridian time).

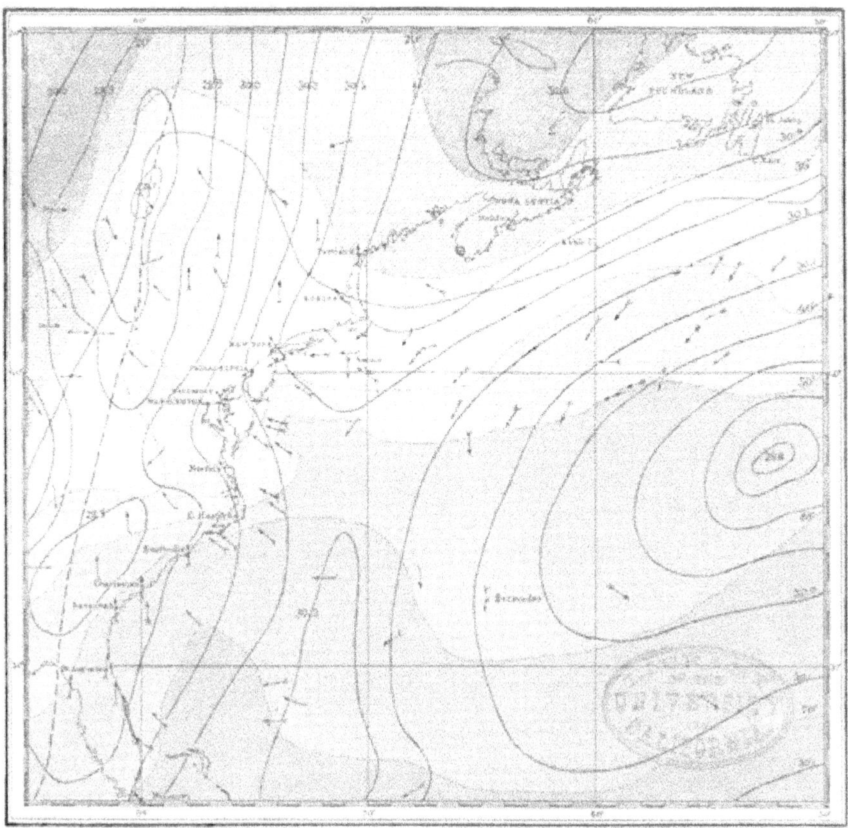

Barometer.—Isobars in full black lines for each tenth of an inch, reduced pressure. The trough of low barometer is shown by a line of dashes.

Temperature.—Isotherms in dotted black lines for each ten degrees Fahr. Temperatures below freezing (32° F.) in shades of blue, and above freezing in red.

Wind.—The small black arrows fly with the wind at the position where each is plotted. The force of wind is indicated in a general way by the number of feathers on the arrows, according to the scale given in the following table:

Plotted on Chart		Force, by scales in practical use.					Pounds per square foot.	Miles per hour.	Kilometers per hour.	Meters per second.
		0 — 12	0 — 10	0 — 8	0 — 7	0 — 6				
O	Calm.	0	0	0	0	0	0	0	0	0
——→	1	1 — 2	1 — 2	1	1 — 2	1	0 — .40	0 — 9	0 — 14.4	0 — 4
——→	2	3 — 4	3 — 4	2	3 — 4	2	0.41 — 2.53	9.1 — 22.5	14.5 — 36.2	4.1 — 10.1
——→	3	5 — 7	5 — 6	3 — 4	5	3	2.54 — 8.50	22.6 — 40.5	36.3 — 65.2	10.2 — 18.1
——→	4	8 — 10	7 — 8	5 — 6	6	4 — 5	8.51 — 25.90	40.6 — 67.5	65.3 — 108.7	18.2 — 30.1
——→	5	11 — 12	9 — 10	7 — 8	7	6	25.91 and over	67.6 and over	108.8 and over	30.2 and over

It will be noticed that the Beaufort scale (0–12), in general use at sea, has been converted into the international scale (0–10) for the sake of clearness in plotting data on the chart. The absence of arrows over large areas indicates absence of simultaneous data; at sea, however, this has been partly compensated for in the construction of the chart by information obtained from journals and special storm reports of vessels in the vicinity.

WEATHER CHART.--MARCH 12.

Meteorological conditions at noon, Greenwich mean time (7 A. M., 75th meridian time).

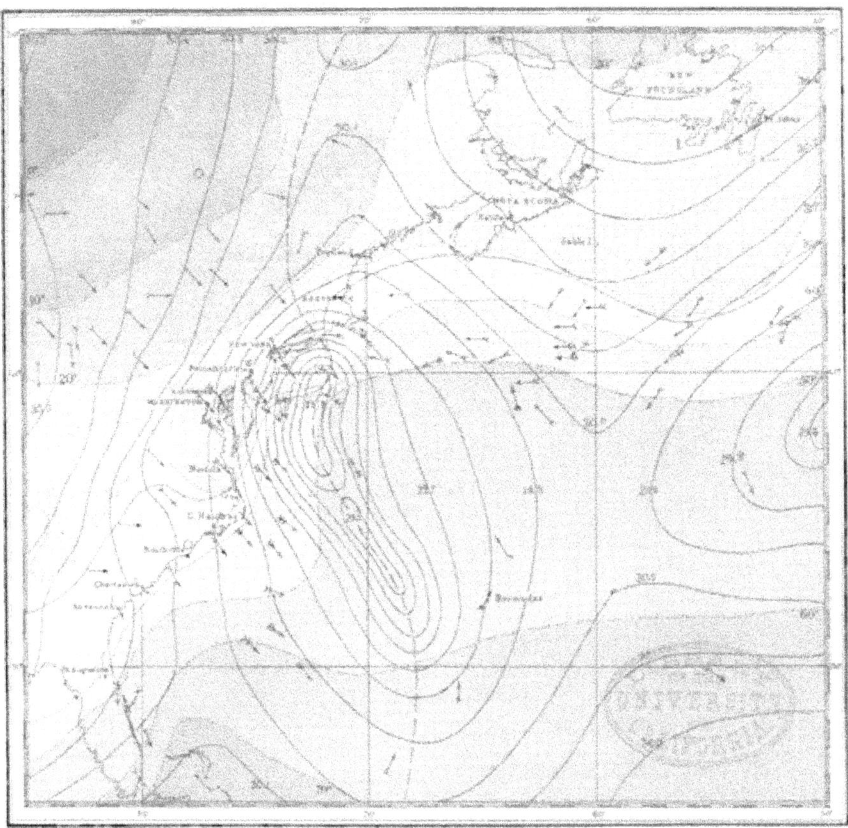

Barometer.—Isobars in full black lines for each tenth of an inch, reduced pressure. The trough of low barometer is shown by a line of dashes.

Temperature.—Isotherms in dotted black lines for each ten degrees Fahr. Temperatures below freezing (32° F.) in shades of blue, and above freezing in red.

Wind.—The small black arrows fly with the wind at the position where each is plotted. The force of wind is indicated in a general way by the number of feathers on the arrows, according to the scale given in the following table:

Plotted on Chart.	Force, by scales in practical use.					Pounds per square foot.	Miles per hour.	Kilometers per hour.	Meters per second.
	0 – 12	0 – 10	0 – 8	0 – 7	0 – 6				
○ Calm.	0	0	0	0	0	0	0	0	0
1	1 – 2	1 – 2	1	1 – 2	1	0 – .40	0 – 9	0 – 14.4	0 – 4
2	3 – 4	3 – 4	2	3 – 4	2	0.41 – 2.50	9.1 – 22.5	14.5 – 36.2	4.1 – 10.1
3	5 – 7	5 – 6	3 – 4	5	3	2.56 – 6.70	22.6 – 40.5	36.3 – 65.2	10.2 – 18.1
4	8 – 10	7 – 8	5 – 6	6	4 – 5	6.71 – 22.00	40.6 – 67.5	65.3 – 108.7	18.2 – 30.1
5	11 – 12	9 – 10	7 – 8	7	6	22.01 and over	67.6 and over	108.8 and over	30.2 and over

It will be noticed that the Beaufort scale (0–12), in general use at sea, has been converted into the international scale (0–10) for the sake of clearness in plotting data on the chart. The absence of arrows over large areas indicates absence of simultaneous data; at sea, however, this has been partly compensated for in the construction of the chart by information obtained from journals and special storm reports of vessels in the vicinity.

WEATHER CHART.--MARCH 13.

Meteorological conditions at noon, Greenwich mean time (7 A. M., 75th meridian time).

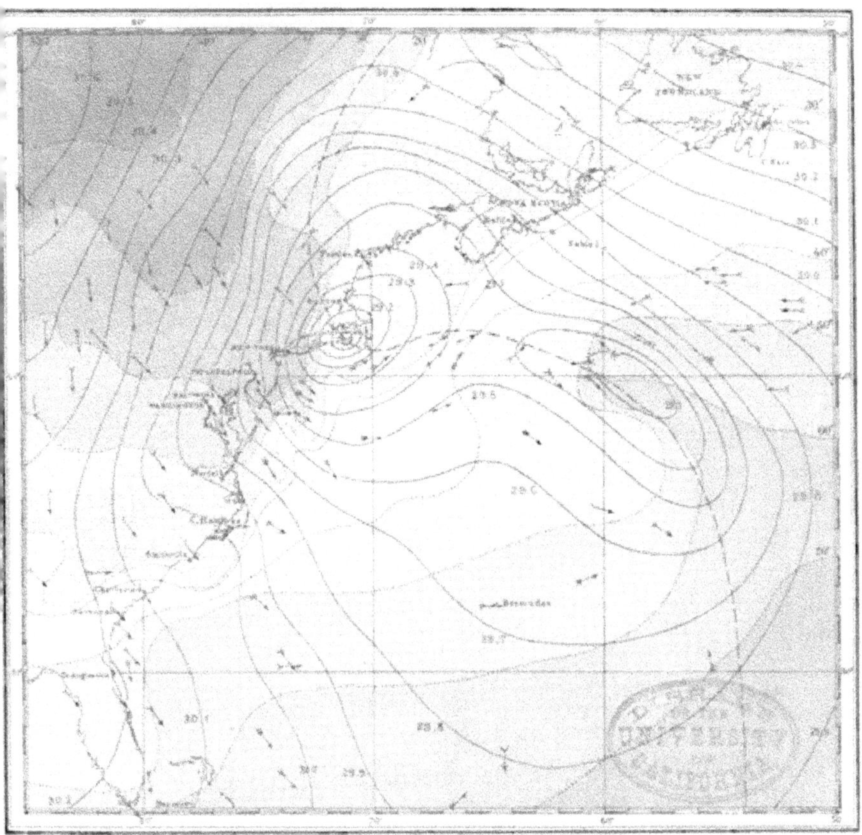

Barometer.—Isobars in full black lines for each tenth of an inch, reduced pressure. The trough of low barometer is shown by a line of dashes.

Temperature.—Isotherms in dotted black lines for each ten degrees Fahr. Temperatures below freezing (32° F.) in shades of blue, and above freezing in red.

Wind.—The small black arrows fly with the wind at the position where each is plotted. The force of wind is indicated in a general way by the number of feathers on the arrows, according to the scale given in the following table:

Plotted on Chart.	Force, by scales in practical use					Pounds per square foot.	Miles per hour.	Kilometers per hour.	Meters per second.
	0 — 12	0 — 10	0 — 9	0 — 7	0 — 6				
O Calm	0	0	0	0	0	0.	0.	0	0.
1	1 — 2	1 — 2	1	1 — 2	1	0. — .40	0 — 9.	0 — 14.4	0 — 4
2	3 — 4	3 — 4	2	3 — 4	2	0.41 — 2.52	9.1 — 22.3	14.5 — 35.9	4.1 — 10.1
3	5 — 7	5 — 6	3 — 4	5	3	2.54 — 8.20	22.4 — 40.3	36.0 — 64.8	10.2 — 18.1
4	8 — 10	7 — 8	5 — 6	6	4 — 5	8.21 — 22.50	40.4 — 67.1	65.0 — 108.0	18.2 — 30.1
5	11 — 12	9 — 10	7 — 9	7	6	22.51 and over.	67.2 and over.	108.1 and over.	30.2 and over.

It will be noticed that the Beaufort scale (0-12), in general use at sea, has been converted into the international scale (0-10) for the sake of clearness in plotting data on the chart. The absence of arrows over large areas indicates absence of simultaneous data; at sea, however, this has been partly compensated for in the construction of the chart by information obtained from journals and special storm reports of vessels in the vicinity.

WEATHER CHART.--MARCH 14.

Meteorological conditions at noon, Greenwich mean time (7 A. M., 75th meridian time).

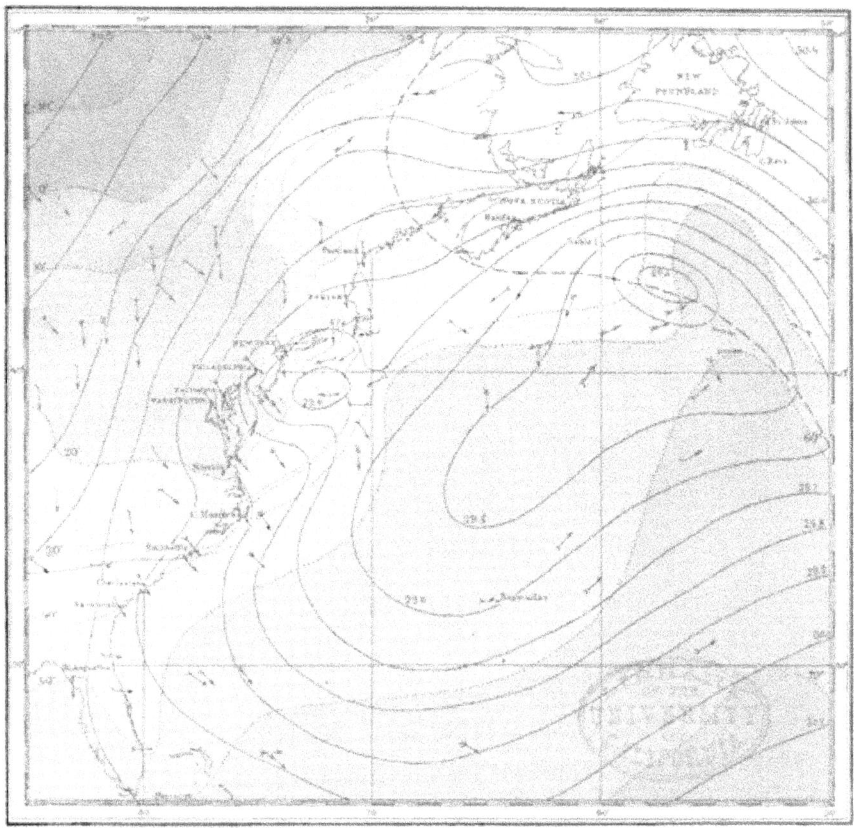

Barometer.—Isobars in full black lines for each tenth of an inch, reduced pressure. The trough of low barometer is shown by a line of dashes.

Temperature.—Isotherms in dotted black lines for each ten degrees Fahr. Temperatures below freezing (32° F.) in shades of blue, and above freezing in red.

Wind.—The small black arrows fly with the wind at the position where each is plotted. The force of wind is indicated in a general way by the number of feathers on the arrows, according to the scale given in the following table:

Plotted on Chart.	Force, by Scales in practical use.					Pounds per square foot.	Miles per hour.	Kilometers per hour.	Meters per second.
	0 — 12	0 — 10	0 — 8	0 — 7	0 — 6				
O Calm.	0	0	0	0	0	0.	0.	0.	0.
1	1 — 2	1 — 2	1	1 — 2	1	0. — .40	0 — 9	0 — 14.5	0 — 4
2	3 — 4	3 — 4	2	3 — 4	2	0.41 — 2.53	9.1 — 22.5	14.6 — 36.2	4.1 — 10.1
3	5 — 7	5 — 6	3 — 4	5	3	2.54 — 8.20	22.6 — 40.5	36.3 — 65.2	10.2 — 18.1
4	8 — 10	7 — 8	5 — 6	6	4 — 5	8.21 — 22.78	40.6 — 67.5	65.3 — 108.7	18.2 — 30.1
5	11 — 12	9 — 10	7 — 8	7	6	22.79 and over	67.6 and over	108.8 and over	30.2 and over

It will be noticed that the Beaufort scale (0–12), in general use at sea, has been converted into the international scale (0–10) for the sake of clearness in plotting data on the chart. The absence of arrows over large areas indicates absence of simultaneous data; at sea, however, this has been partly compensated for in the construction of the chart by information obtained from journals and special storm reports of vessels in the vicinity.

TRACK CHART.

Positions of the trough of low barometer and tracks of vessels, March 11-14, 1888.

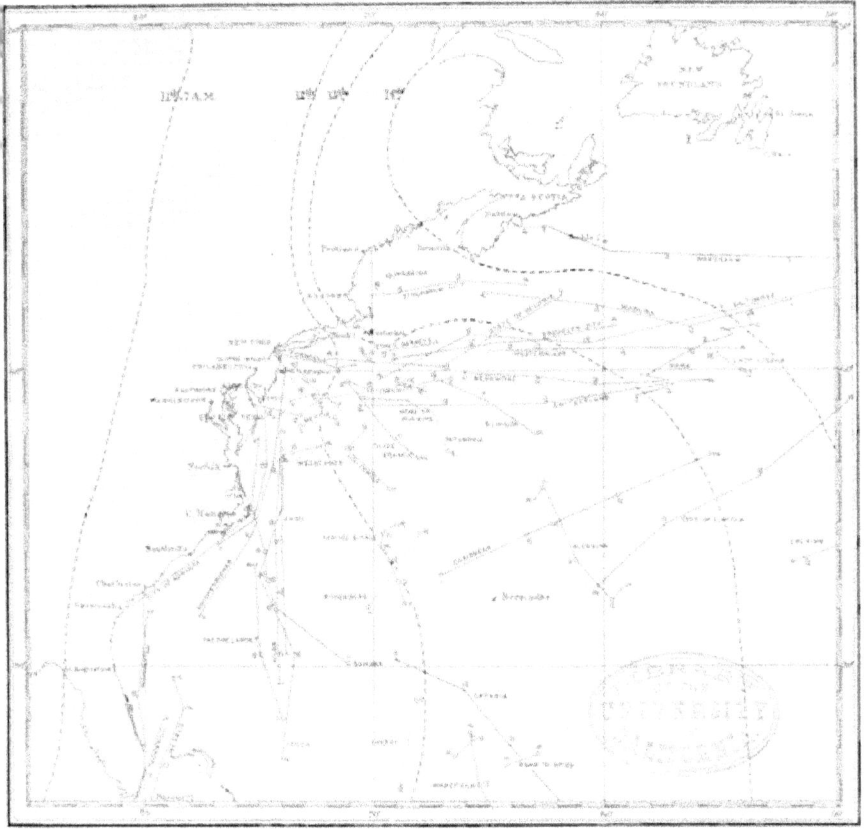

Positions at 7 A. M. (Greenwich noon) are indicated on the chart by a point; at noon, ship's time, by a small circle.

Black.—The line of dashes indicates the position of the trough of low barometer, or the line of sudden change from easterly to westerly winds, with brief intervals of calm, shifts of wind in heavy squalls of rain or snow, colder, and, finally, clearing weather.

Red.—Positions and names of land stations and names and tracks of vessels plotted in red are those whose barometer curves are shown in the accompanying Barometer Diagram.

Blue.—The tracks of certain other vessels from which storm reports have been received are plotted **in blue**. In addition to these, however, storm reports have been received from the following vessels, omitted from the chart in order to avoid confusion:

Transatlantic steamships, westward bound: Glenderon, Lydian Monarch, St. Ronans, Wera.

Coasting steamships, bound south: El Monte, Morgan City, New Orleans. *Bound north:* Newport.

Sailing vessels off the coast from Montauk point to [illegible]*:* Spartan, Charles H. Marshall, [illegible], John H. [illegible], [illegible], Iroquois, [illegible], Warren B. Potter, Normandy, [illegible], Melissa Trask, Wilhelm [illegible], Johanna, [illegible].

BAROMETER DIAGRAM.

Illustrating the fluctuations of the barometer from noon, March 11, to noon, March 14 (75th meridian time).

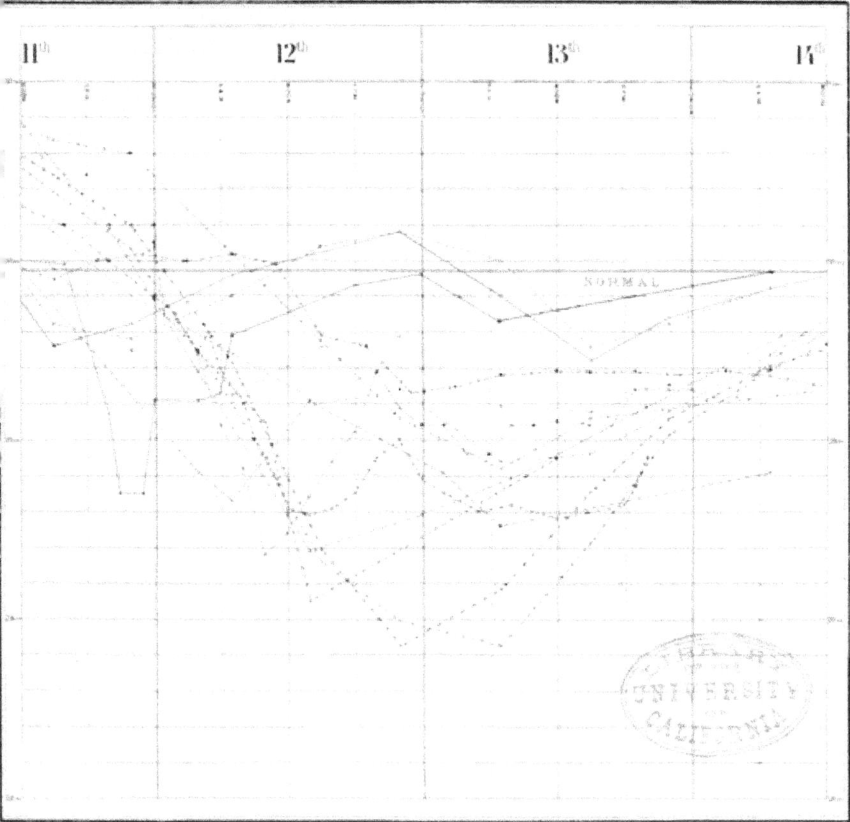

Barometer **Curves.**—As it is only practicable to illustrate graphically the barometer records of a few vessels and land stations, the following have been selected as being of special interest, the small circles mark the points of observation;

SIGNAL STATIONS.	VESSELS.
Norfolk.	British steamship Andes.
Hatteras.	American schooner Kennett.
Atlantic City.	British steamship Lord Clive.
New York.	American schooner Lida Fowler.
Block Island.	American schooner George Walker
Nantucket.	British steamship Serapis.
Yarmouth, N. S.	British ship Glenburn.

Barometer Normal.—The barometer normal for the 5°-square from latitude 35° to 40° N., longitude 65° to 70° W., assumed for the present purpose as the normal for the entire area, is 29.98, and is indicated by the blue line on the diagram.

The positions of the above-mentioned signal-stations and the tracks of these seven vessels are all indicated in red on the accompanying Track Chart. This diagram should therefore be studied in connection with the chart, in order to form a clear idea of the general eastward movement of the trough of low barometer, and the accompanying rapid deepening of the depression upon reaching the coast.

TABLE OF CONTENTS.

CHAPTER I.

INTRODUCTION.

The history of a great ocean storm can not be written with any completeness until a long interval of time has elapsed, when the meteorological observations taken on board hundreds of vessels of every nationality, scattered over the broad expanse of ocean, and bound, many of them, for far distant ports, can be gathered together, compared, and, where observations seem discordant, rigidly analyzed and the best data selected. It is only when based upon such a foundation that the story can fully deserve the title of history, and not romance—fact, and not hypothesis. At best there must be wide areas where the absence of vessels will forever leave some blank pages in this history, while elsewhere, along the great highways of ocean traffic, the data are absolutely complete. Last August a tropical hurricane of terrific violence swept in toward our coast from between Bermuda and the Bahamas, curved to the northward off Hatteras, and continued its destructive course past the Grand Banks toward Northern Europe. Hundreds of reports from masters of vessels enabled us accurately to plot its track, a great parabolic curve tangent to St. Thomas, Hatteras, Cape Race, and the northern coast of Norway. Six months later a report forwarded by the British meteorological office, from a vessel homeward bound from the equator, indicated that it originated far to the eastward, off the coast of Africa; and only the other day the log of the British ship *Glenburn*, Captain Johansen, at New York, March 30, from Calcutta, supplied data by means of which the storm track can be traced still more accurately westward of the Cape Verde islands. Not only that, but this same vessel on the 11th of March was about 500 miles to the eastward of Bermuda, and while the great storm was raging between Hatteras and Sandy Hook was traversing a region to the northeastward of Bermuda, from which our records are as yet very incomplete. It will thus be clearly understood that while the most earnest efforts have been made not only to collect and utilize all available information but to be careful and cautious in generalizing from the data at hand, yet this study must be considered as only preliminary to an exhaustive treatise based on more complete data than it is now possible to obtain.

Four charts have been prepared to illustrate the meteorological conditions within the area from 25° to 50° north latitude, 50° to 85° west longitude, at 7 a. m., seventy-fifth meridian time, March 11, 12, 13, and 14, respectively. Data for land stations have been taken from the daily weather maps published by the U. S. Signal Service, and the set of tri-daily maps covering the period of the great storm has been invaluable for reference throughout this discussion. Marine data are from reports of marine meteorology made to this office by masters of vessels, and not only from vessels within the area charted, but from many others just beyond its limits. The refined and accurate observations taken with standard instruments at the same moment of absolute time all over the United States by the skilled observers of the Signal Service, together with those contributed to the Hydrographic Office by the voluntary co-operation of masters of vessels of every nationality, and taken with instruments compared with standards at the branch hydrographic offices immediately upon arrival in port, make it safe to say that never have the data been so complete and reliable for such a discussion at such an early date.

It will not be out of place briefly to refer here to certain principles of meteorology that are essential to a clear understanding of what follows. The general atmospheric movement in these latitudes is from west to east, and by far the greater proportion of all the areas of low barometer, or centers of more or less perfectly developed wind systems, that traverse the United States move along paths which cross the Great Lakes, and thence reach out over the Gulf of St. Lawrence across the Atlantic toward Iceland and northern Europe. Another very characteristic storm path may also be referred to in this connection, the curved track along which West Indian hurricanes travel up the coast. The atmospheric movement in the tropics is, generally speaking, westward, but a hurricane starting on a westward track soon curves off to the northwest and north, and then, getting into the general eastward trend of the temperate zone, falls into line and moves off to the northeast, circling about the area of high barometer which so persistently overhangs the Azores and a great elliptical area to the southwestward. The circulation of the wind about these areas of low barometer and the corresponding changes of temperature are indicated graphically on the daily weather map; the isobars, or lines of equal barometric pressure, are, as a rule, somewhat circular in form, and the winds blow about and away from an area of "high" in a direction *with the hands of a watch* (in nautical parlance, "with the sun"), toward and about "low," with an opposite rotary motion, or against the hands of a watch; in front of a "low" there will therefore be, in general, warm southeasterly winds, and behind it cold northwesterly winds, the resulting changes of temperature being shown by the isotherms, or lines of equal temperature. Moreover, in a cyclonic system of this kind the westerly winds are generally far stronger than the easterly winds, the motion of the whole system from west to east increasing the apparent force of the former and decreasing that of the latter. Upon reaching the coast such areas of low barometer, or storm systems, almost invariably develop a great increase of energy, largely due to the moisture in the atmosphere overhanging the ocean, which, when the air is chilled by contact with the cold, dry air rushing in from the "high," is precipitated and becomes visible in the form of clouds, with rain or snow. The latent heat liberated by the condensation of this aqueous vapor plays a most important part in the continuance of the storm's energy, and indeed in its increase of energy; the warm, li ht air, flowing in toward the central area of the storm, rises rapidly into regions where the pressure is less, that is, where the thickness and consequently the weight of the superincumbent atmosphere is less; it therefore rapidly expands, and such expansion would result in a much more rapid cooling and a corresponding decrease in its tendency to rise still higher, were it not for the latent heat liberated by the condensation of the moisture which it contains. Thus the forces that are conspiring to increase the energy of the storm are powerfully assisted by the presence and condensation of aqueous vapor, and the increasing up-draught and rarefaction are at once marked by the decreasing barometric pressure at the center. For example, a storm was central over the Great Lakes on January 25, with lowest barometer 29.7; the following day it was central off Nantucket, barometer 29.2; and on the 27th and 28th over the Gulf of St. Lawrence, with barometer below 28.6. But such instances are so common as to make it the rule and not the exception. As stated above, the isobars about an area of low barometer are somewhat circular in form; more strictly speaking, they are somewhat oval or elliptical in shape, and the more elongated the north and south axis of this ellipse the greater the resulting changes of temperature, because as it moves along its broad path toward the Atlantic the in-draught, or suction, is felt in front far down toward the tropics, and in rear far to the northward, beyond the territorial limits of the United States.

Similarly with regard to the general movement of areas of high barometer, certain laws of motion have been clearly established by means of studies of the daily international charts; instead of a motion toward east-northeast, these areas, when north of the fortieth parallel, have in general a motion towards east-southeast, and as a rule move more rapidly and with greater momentum than "lows," so that they may be said to have the right of way when the tracks of two such systems converge or intersect. These laws, or at least that relating to the Great Lake storm track, as it may be called, soon become evident to anyone who watches the weather map from day to day, upon which are charted the systems of low and high barometer as they follow one another across the continent, bringing each its characteristic weather.

CHAPTER II.

MARCH 11, 7 A. M.

The first of the accompanying weather charts indicates graphically the meteorological conditions over the wide area charted, comprising about 3,000,000 square miles, of which one-third is land and two-thirds water. Over the land there is a long line or trough of low barometer, extending from the west coast of Florida up past the eastern shore of Lake Huron and far northward toward the southern limits of Hudson Bay. In front of this advancing line the prevailing winds are southeasterly, and the warm moist air drawn up from southern latitudes spreads a warm wave along the coast, with generally cloudy weather and heavy rains, especially south of Hatteras; the Signal Service observer at Pensacola, for example, reports the heavy fall of 4.05 inches on the 10th. About midway of this trough of low barometer there is a long, narrow region of light, variable winds; of rapid changes in meteorological conditions; calms, shifts of wind, intervals of clearing weather; then overcast again, with cooler weather, and fresh northwesterly winds, increasing to a gale. The front line of this advancing battalion of cold northwesterly winds is more than a thousand miles in length, and covers the whole breadth of the United States; its right flank is on the Gulf, its left rests on the Great Lakes, or even farther north; the temperature falls rapidly at its approach, with frost far south into Louisiana and Mississippi, and heavy snow in central Kentucky and eastern Tennessee. The long swaying line is advancing toward the coast at the rate of about 600 miles a day, followed by a ridge of high barometer reaching from Texas to Dakota and Manitoba. At points along the trough the barometer ranges from 29.70, a hundred miles north of Toronto, to 29.86 at Pittsburgh, 29.88 at Augusta, and 29.94 at Cedar Keys. Along the ridge the barometer is very high; 30.7 to the northward about Lake Winnipeg, 30.6 in Wyoming, 30.7 in Indian Territory, and 30.5 south of the Rio Grande. The difference of pressure from trough to ridge is thus measured by about an inch of mercury in the barometer. Moreover, the chart shows that there is another ridge of high barometer in advance, curving down off the coast from northern Newfoundland, where the pressure is 30.6, toward Santo Domingo, where it is about 30.3, and passing midway between Hatteras and Bermuda. Farther to the eastward the concentric isobars show the presence of a storm which originated about Bermuda on the 9th, and is moving off toward Europe, where, in a few days, it may cause northwesterly gales with snow to the northward of its track, and southeasterly gales with rain to the southward. Storm reports from the steam-ships *Erl King* and *Glenderon*, the ships *Glenburn* and *Anna*, and the brig *Olive Branch* show that this storm was of hurricane violence, with heavy squalls and high seas; but it need not be referred to in this connection further than to say that it sent back a long, rolling swell from northeast, felt all along the Atlantic sea-board the morning of the 11th, and quite distinct from that caused by the freshening gale from the southeast.

CHAPTER III.

METEOROLOGICAL CONDITIONS OFF THE COAST.

While this great trough of low barometer, with all its attendant phenomena, is advancing rapidly eastward toward the Atlantic, and the cold wave in its train is spreading over towns, counties, and states, crossing the Great Lakes, moving up the Ohio Valley, and extending far south over the Gulf of Mexico, we may pause for a moment to consider a factor which is to play a most important part in the warfare of the elements so soon to rage with destructive violence between Hatteras and Block Island, and finally to disturb the weather of the entire North Atlantic north of the twentieth parallel.

The great warm ocean current called the Gulf Stream has, to most people, a more or less vague, mythical existence. The words sound familiar, but the thing itself is only an abstract idea; it lacks reality, for want of any personal experience or knowledge of its characteristic effects. To the navigator of the North Atlantic it is a reality; it has a concrete, definite existence; it is an element which enters into the calculations of his every-day life—sometimes as a friend, to help him on his course, sometimes as an enemy, to endanger, harass, and delay. Briefly, the warm waters of the tropics are carried slowly and steadily westward by the broad equatorial drift-current and banked up in the Caribbean Sea and Gulf of Mexico, there to constitute the head or source of the Gulf Stream, by which the greater portion is drained off through the straits of Florida in a comparatively narrow and swiftly moving stream. This great movement goes on unceasingly, subject, however, to certain variations which the changing seasons bring with them. As the sun advances northward in the spring, the southeast trades creep up toward and across the equator, the volume of that portion of the equatorial current which is diverted to the northward of Cape San Roque is gradually increased, and this increase is soon felt far to the westward in the Yucatan and Florida Straits. Figures fail utterly to give even an approximate idea of the amount of heat thus conveyed from the tropics to the north temperate zone by the ceaseless pulsations of this mighty engine of oceanic circulation. To put it in some tangible shape for the mind to grasp, however, suppose we consider the amount of energy in the form of heat that would be liberated were this great volume of water reduced in temperature to the freezing point. Suppose, again, that we convert the number of heat-units thus obtained into units of work, so many foot-pounds, and thence ascertain the corresponding horse-power, in order to compare it with something with which we are familiar. Considering only the portion of the Gulf Stream that flows between Cape Florida and the Great Bahama Bank, we find from the latest and most reliable data, collected by the U. S. Coast and Geodetic Survey, that the area of cross section is 10.97 square miles (geographic or sea miles of 6,080 feet each); mean velocity at this time of the year, 1.305 miles per hour; mean temperature, 71° F. These figures for mean velocity and temperature from surface to bottom are, it will be noticed, far below those for the surface current alone, where the velocity is often as great as 5 knots an hour and the temperature as high as 80°. The indicated horse-power of a great ocean steam-ship—*La Bourgogne*, *Werra*, *Umbria*, and *City of New York*, for example—is from 9,000 to 16,000; that of some modern vessels of war is still greater; the *Vulcan*, now building for the British Government, is 20,000, and the *Sardegna*, for the Italian Government, 22,800.

Again, if we convert into its equivalent horse-power the potential energy of the 270,000 cubic feet of water per second which rush down the rapids of Niagara and make their headlong plunge of 160 feet over the American and Horse-Shoe Falls, we get the enormous sum of 5,847,000. The Gulf Stream, however, is every hour carrying north through the straits of Florida 14½ cubic miles of water (more than three thousand times the volume of Niagara), equivalent, considering the amount of heat it contains from 71° to 32° F., to *three trillion and sixty-three billion horse-power*, or more than five hundred thousand times as much as all of these combined; indeed, considering only the amount of heat from 71° to 50°, it is still two hundred and seventy-five thousand times as great.

Sweeping northward toward Hatteras with its widening torrent, its volume still further increased by new supplies drawn in from about the Bahamas and the northern coast of Cuba, its color a limpid ultramarine, like the dark blue of the Mediterranean or of some deep mountain lake, it then spreads northeastward toward the Grand Banks of Newfoundland, and with decreasing velocity and lower temperature gradually merges in the general easterly drift that sets toward the shores of Europe about the fortieth parallel.

The cold inshore current must also be considered, because it is to great contrasts of temperature that the violence of storms is very largely due. East of Newfoundland the Labrador current flows southward, and during the spring and summer months carries gigantic icebergs and masses of field-ice into the tracks of transatlantic steam-ships. Upon meeting the Gulf Stream a portion of this cold current underruns it and continues on its course at the bottom of the sea; another portion is deflected to the southwest and flows, counter to the Gulf Stream, along the coast as far south as Hatteras.

The broad features of these great ocean currents have thus been briefly outlined, and, although they are subject to considerable variation as to temperature, velocity, and limits, in response to the varying forces that act upon them, this general review must suffice for the present purpose.

Now to consider for a moment some of the phenomena resulting from the presence and relative positions of these ocean currents, so far as such phenomena bear upon the great storm now under consideration. With the Pilot Chart of the North Atlantic Ocean for March there was issued a supplement descriptive of waterspouts off the Atlantic coast of the United States during January and February. Additional interest and importance have been given to the facts there grouped together and published by their evident bearing upon the conditions which gave rise to the tremendous increase of violence attendant upon the approach of this trough of low barometer toward the coast. In it were given descriptions, in greater or less detail, of as many as forty waterspouts reported by masters of vessels during these two months, at various positions off the coast, from the northern coast of Cuba to the Grand Banks; and since that supplement was published many other similar reports have been received. Moreover, it was pointed out that the conditions that give rise to such remarkable and dangerous phenomena are due to the interaction between the warm, moist air overhanging the Gulf Stream and the cold dry air brought over it by northwesterly winds from the coast and from over the cold inshore current, and the greater the difference of temperature and moisture the greater the resulting energy of action. Reports were also quoted showing that the Gulf Stream was beginning to reassert itself after a period of comparative quiescence during the winter months, and with increasing strength and volume was approaching its northern limits as the sun moved north in declination. By way of more vividly illustrating the violence of the energy thus developed, a few of these reports may well be quoted here.

Captain Dexter, American steam-ship *City of Para*, saw several large spouts, January 22, about 300 miles east from Savannah. Three huge spouts were seen at once, and six in the course of half an hour. The water seemed to be drawn up from the sea, mounting in spiral columns of tremendous thickness, with a loud roaring sound.

Captain Cleary, British steam-ship *River* [illegible], states that on January 28, latitude 39.30 N., longitude 57.20 W., he saw what he took to be a heavy squall to the southeast. Upon looking at it with his glass he saw that it was a whirlwind, raising the water to a great height. It must have been over a mile in diameter, but he hesitates even to estimate the height to which the water was raised or the size of the spout, although it must have had terrific power.

The American bark *Reindeer*, Captain Strandt, was, on the morning of February 11, about 300 miles west of Bermuda, running to the northward with a fair wind and all sail set. The vessel was suddenly struck by a waterspout; all her masts went over the side with a crash, with yards, sails, standing rigging, and running gear. The force of the blow shattered the immense column of water, which luckily did not fall upon her decks, or it might have resulted in loss of life. The crew were paralyzed with fear, hardly knowing what had happened, so sudden was the shock.

Finally, the British steam-ship *Paronia*, Captain McKay, was off the Grand Banks (latitude 41.59 N., longtitude 47.32 W.) April 10, when a large spout formed to the southwest and traveled to the northeast at the rate of about 30 miles an hour. The vessel's course was changed to avoid it. As it passed, the whirling rush of air was felt on board. The great column of water reached up to a dense low-lying cloud, and was in shape like a huge hour-glass. It was accompanied by a terrific roaring, and the water at its base was churned into a mass of foam, causing such a commotion that it made the great ocean steam-ship tremble. When off the starboard bow the spout broke, with vivid lightning, heavy thunder, and a deluge of rain and hail, some of the pieces of ice being from four to six inches in diameter.

Such, then, were the meteorological conditions off the coast awaiting the attack of the advance guard of this long line of cold northwesterly gales—conditions still further intensified by the freshening gale that sprung up from the southeast at its approach, drawing re-enforcements of warm, moist ocean air from far down within the tropics. The few reports which have been quoted illustrate the intensity of the energy developed when storm systems of only ordinary character and severity reach the Atlantic on their eastward march toward northern Europe. Let us now return to the consideration of this storm which is advancing toward the coast at the rate of about 600 miles a day, in the form of a great arched squall whose front is more than a thousand miles in length, and which is followed, far down the line, by northwesterly gales and temperatures below the freezing point.

CHAPTER IV.

THE NIGHT OF MARCH 11-12.

Sunday afternoon at 3 o'clock the line of the storm center, or trough, extended in a curved line, convex to the east, from Lake Ontario down through New York State and Pennsylvania, along about the middle of Chesapeake Bay to Norfolk, across North Carolina to Point Lookout, and thence down through eastern Florida to Key West.

Northeasterly, easterly, and southeasterly gales were therefore felt all along the coast from the Gulf of St. Lawrence to the Florida Keys, except in the bight between Lookout and Cañaveral, where the barometer had reached and passed its lowest point, and the wind was northwest, with much cooler weather. Reference to the Barometer Diagram shows pretty clearly that the trough passed Norfolk a short time before it reached Hatteras, where the lowest reading was undoubtedly lower the evening of the 11th than it was at Norfolk.

By 10 p. m. the line has advanced as far east as the seventy-fourth meridian. Telegraphic reports are soon all in from signal stations along the coast. The barometer is rising at Hatteras and Norfolk and still falling at Atlantic City, New York, and Block Island, but there is little or no indication of the fury of the storm off shore along the seventy-fourth meridian, from the thirtieth to the fortieth parallel, where the cold northwesterly gale is sweeping over the great warm ocean current, carrying air at a temperature below the freezing point over water above 75° F., and where the barometer is falling more and more rapidly, the gale becoming a storm and the storm a hurricane. Nor are there any indications that the area of high barometer about Newfoundland is slowing down, blocking the advance of the rapidly increasing storm and about to hold the center of the line in check to the westward of Nantucket for days, which seem like weeks, while a terrific northwest gale plays havoc along the coast from Montauk Point to Hatteras, and until the right flank of the line has swung around to the eastward far enough to cut off the supply of warm, moist air pouring in from the southeast. Long before midnight the welcome "good night" message has flashed along the wires to all the signal stations from the Atlantic to the Pacific slope, whilst at sea, aboard scores of vessels, from the little fishing-schooner and pilot boat to the great transatlantic liner, a life-or-death struggle with the elements is being waged, with heroism none the less real because it is in self-defense and none the less admirable because it can not always avert disaster.

The accompanying Track Chart gives the tracks of as many vessels as can be shown without confusion, and illustrates very clearly where data for this discussion are most complete, as well as where additional information is specially needed. Thus it is here plainly evident that vessels are always most numerous to the eastward of New York (along the transatlantic route) and to the southward, off the coast. To the southeastward, however, about the Bermudas, there is a large area from which comparatively few reports have been received, although additional data will doubtless be obtained from outward-bound sailing vessels, upon their return. Of all the days in the week, Saturday, in particular, is the day on which the greatest number of vessels sail from New York. The 10th of March, for instance, as many as eight transatlantic liners got under way: The *Aurania*, *City of Chester*, and *Brooklyn City*, for Liverpool, *La Normandie* for Havre, the *Sorrento* for Hamburg, the *Elbe* for Bremen, the *Amsterdam* for Rotterdam, and the *Westernland* for

Antwerp; southward-bound, the *Finance* sailed for Rio, the *Colon* for Aspinwall, the *Andes* for Cartagena, *El Monte* and *New Orleans* for New Orleans, and the *Old Dominion* and *Roanoke* for Chesapeake Bay. Out in mid-ocean there were plowing their way toward our coast, to encounter the storm west of the fiftieth meridian, the *Wandrahm* for Halifax; the *Bulgarian*, *Carthaginian*, *Kansas*, *Madura*, and *Glenderon*, for Boston; the *Alaska*, *Furnessia*, *Celtic*, *Switzerland*, *Werra*, *La Gascogne*, *Slavonia*, *Nederland*, *St. Ronans*. *Benison*, *State of Georgia*, *Lydian Monarch*, *Edam*, *Egypt*, *France*, *The Queen*, *Bohemia*, *City of San Antonio*, and *Serapis*, for New York; the *Lord Clive* for Philadelphia, the *Baltimore* for Baltimore, and the *City of Lincoln* and *Erl King* for New Orleans. Northward-bound, off the coast, were the *Samana*, *Faedrelandet*, *State of Texas*, *Newport*, *Ailsa*, and *Knickerbocker*, not to mention here the many sailing vessels engaged in the coasting or foreign trade, whose sails whiten the waters of our coasts.

Fully to understand the reports that are quoted it will be well to refer to the chart and consider each vessel's position at any given time, relative to the corresponding position of the trough of low barometer. There is no permanency of location about these signal stations of ours at sea, and this fact introduces an element of confusion which should be carefully guarded against. For this reason it is thought that this Track Chart, with vessels' positions plotted for certain dates and times, will be found useful for reference.

Of all the steam-ships that sailed from New York on the 10th, those bound south, with hardly a single exception, encountered the storm in all its fury off the coast. Eastward-bound vessels escaped its greatest violence, although all met with strong head winds and heavy seas, and had the storm not delayed between Block Island and Nantucket on the 12th and 13th would have been overtaken by it off the Grand Banks. Captain Hathorne, American steam-ship *El Monte*, reports that he was so far south as to feel little or nothing of the storm, although he could see that there was a disturbance to the northward. Captain Wetherill, British steam-ship *Thornhill*, encountered a gale from southeast March 10, and the barometer continued to fall, although he was steaming south, until early the following morning, when it was 29.87 about 130 miles east-northeast from Cape Cañaveral. We thus find the energy of the storm increasing already and the barometric pressure deepening, for the lowest recorded barometer reading at Cedar Keys on the 11th was only 29.91, and at Titusville and Jupiter Inlet, 29.88. Indeed, had the *Thornhill* not been moving southward the barometer would undoubtedly have reached a still lower point. This deepening of the depression was still more marked farther north, where the contrasts of temperature were greater. For instance, Captain Stevens, American steam-ship *Manhattan*, encountered a gale from SE. off Cape Romaine, shifting to S., SW. and NW.; highest velocity of wind, about 50 miles per hour, and lowest barometer 29.83, at 4 p. m., 75 miles SE. from Savannah. Captain Gardner, American steam-ship *Morgan City*, passed Hatteras at 7 a. m., bound south; barometer 30.10, wind ESE., force 5, hauling gradually to SSE. and increasing in force; 10 a. m., barometer 29.90, wind SSE., force 8; 5 p. m., 29.50, S., force 10, in squalls, accompanied by a deluge of rain. At 5.30 p. m., when 25 miles S. by E. from Point Lookout, the wind shifted to NNW. and fell to a light breeze. The barometer remained steady till 7 p. m., when it commenced rising. At 10 p. m. the wind had increased in force to 10, moderating the following morning. The American bark *James S. Stone*, Captain Barstow, was off the coast below Hatteras, bound north. At 5 p. m., latitude 32.45 N., longitude 74.45 W., the wind was blowing a strong gale from SSE.; 6 p. m., incessant lightning from S. to NW., wind blowing a furious gale from SSE., with rain and very heavy sea; barometer 29.60. At 8 p. m. the wind died away, leaving the vessel in the trough of a terrible sea; weather thick and rainy; position, about 120 miles SSE. from Hatteras. In an hour the wind blew up in a strong gale from westward and continued for three days between WNW. and NNW., with fierce squalls of hail and sleet; barometer low and unsteady. Captain Catherine, American steam-ship *City of Augusta*, experienced a gale from SE., shifting to S. and NW., highest force, 10, lowest barometer, 29.35, at 1 a. m., off Hatteras. Captain Halsey, American steam-ship *New Orleans*, reports that from noon, off the capes of Chesapeake Bay, to midnight, off Hatteras, the southeasterly breeze increased to a gale, the gale to a furious storm from south (with high seas breaking over the vessel and sweeping the decks fore and aft), shifting at 10 p. m. to a hurricane from NW. The following day the gale moderated slightly, as the vessel steamed south, the sea running very high, and at 6 p. m., when off the Carolina coast below Cape Fear, it cleared up, with fine weather and rising barometer. Captain Williams, American steam-ship *State of Texas*, reports that when abreast of Hatteras Shoals, at 9.30 p. m., northward-bound, the wind, which had been blowing a heavy gale from SE., shifted in a violent squall to NNW., with thunder and lightning, blowing very hard and followed by freezing weather. About 20 miles north of Hatteras Shoals the American schooner *Melissa Trask*, Captain Fletcher, encountered this same violent shift of wind. She had been running north under close-reefed mainsail and staysail, making 8 knots before a strong gale from SSE., with thunder and lightning to the SW. at 8 p. m. At 9.20 p. m. the increasing gale shifted to NNW. very suddenly, moderating for about three minutes and then blowing with terrific force. At 11 p. m. it shifted to NW., with a heavy cross sea, and blew with hurricane force till 7 a. m. of the 12th, when the barometer commenced to rise and the wind moderated to a heavy gale, with snow and hail. The lowest reported reading of her barometer was 29.80, and this report agrees very well with the 10 p. m. weather map published by the Signal Service, although that map does not indicate, for lack of marine data at time of publication, that another marked depression, or secondary, had already formed off shore north of Hatteras, in addition to that which had only just moved eastward from over central Georgia and had passed the coast with increasing energy between Point Lookout and Cape Fear. The fact that the barometer of the *Melissa Trask* remained steady at 29.80 from 10 p. m. till 7 a. m., in spite of the rapid eastward movement of the whole storm system, shows how rapidly the barometric depression was really deepening. The continued low reading may have been partly due, however, to the fact that the vessel was blown off her course about 200 miles to the southeast, thus following the storm. She experienced a continuous gale from NW. to NNW. till the night of the 14th, with a high, confused sea and occasional snow and hail.

About 50 miles NNE. from Hatteras Captain Kinney, American bark *Lottie Stewart*, reports that at 10 p. m. the wind shifted suddenly from SE. to NW., blowing very hard and increasing toward midnight to a terrific hurricane, with blinding rain, blowing away both topsails and breaking yards. The barometer had fallen from 30.02 at noon to 29.62 at 10 o'clock. It continued to blow very hard, with low barometer, till the morning of the 12th, the vessel lying perfectly helpless in the heavy sea, and drifting southeastward across the Gulf Stream. The weather cleared up a little on the 12th, with rising barometer, which at 2 p. m. on the 13th had risen to 29.92, when it began to fall again, and on the 14th the gale increased from the northward, with heavy snow squalls, followed finally by rising barometer and fine weather. This second fall of the barometer is fully explained by reference to the weather charts of the 12th and 13th, and will be referred to again later on.

A little farther northward we have a report from Captain Richardson, American schooner *Nantucket*, who gives a lowest barometric reading of 29.50 at 10 p. m., 70 miles east from Cape Henry. He calls special attention to the fact that for the first twelve hours, and indeed for nearly twenty-four hours, the barometer vibrated in the most remarkable way, as much as .13 at a time, which well attests the violence of the squalls attending the formation of the secondary storm center mentioned above, as well as the increasing severity of the entire storm. The velocity of the wind, he estimates, was as high as 100 miles per hour.

The above report is sustained very well by the following from Captain Andrews, American schooner *Warren B. Potter*, who had passed within 20 miles of Hatteras at 11 a. m., bound north, strong breeze from SE., overcast and rainy, falling barometer. The wind increased gradually in force, but remained steady at SE. till 11 p. m., when it shifted suddenly to WNW., throwing everything aback. Had reduced sail, expecting heavy weather, as the barometer had been falling all day and the wind increasing. In a few minutes the wind hauled to NW.; overcast and black overhead, so dark could not make out clouds; occasional lightning and heavy thunder; high sea from SE., which broke on board and did considerable damage. Lowest barometer 29.40; position (estimated), 50 miles E. by S. from Cape Henry.

Off Henlopen we have a very interesting report from Captain Norton, sailing master of the 88 ton steel schooner-yacht *Iroquois*, owned by Mr. T. Jefferson Coolidge, of Boston. The *Iroquois* passed Sandy Hook the afternoon of the 10th, bound south. The next day the wind continued to freshen from SE., with falling barometer, sea increasing fast; 10 p. m., wind increasing and canting southeasterly, occasional rain squalls, and weather looking bad, especially to the NW.; 11.40 p. m., wind shifted suddenly to NW. in a squall blowing very hard, but nothing to what came later on; by 1 a. m. it had increased to a most terrific gale, blowing at the rate of 60 or 70 miles an hour.

A few miles to the northwestward of the *Iroquois* the American brig *Arcot*, Captain Cates, was lying-to off Five-Fathom Bank light-ship, in an easterly storm and heavy cross sea from NE. and ESE.; barometer 29.20 (apparently this reading is .3 too low for this position the evening of the 11th). At 1 a. m. she was struck by a violent hurricane with blinding snow from NNW., completely overwhelming the vessel in a wild, confused sea which blew half mast high. To save his vessel from swamping, Captain Cates had to bear off before the gale, which blew at the rate of 80 or 90 miles an hour for twenty-four hours, with steady snow and hail. Hundreds of land-birds were about the vessel, struggling in the gale and dropping into the sea. On the 13th the wind backed to NW. by N., blowing a whole gale, with heavy squalls of snow and hail, for forty-eight hours, followed by a fresh gale from WNW. for thirty-six hours more.

Last, but by no means least, in our glance along the coast this memorable night, let us look off Barnegat and Sandy Hook, where the shift of wind came later, but with still greater violence, fiercer squalls, lower temperature, and more blinding snow.

The American bark *Coryphene*, Captain Grosse, at noon of the 11th was off the capes of the Delaware, bound north. Beautiful weather and moderate easterly breeze, but the barometer, which had previously been very high, was now falling slowly. During the afternoon it became hazy about the horizon, the wind increased, the barometer fell more rapidly, and it commenced raining, the weather getting thick and threatening; 6 p. m., 28 fathoms of water, wind very unsteady, sometimes inclined to haul to S., sometimes to N., moderately high sea from eastward; 8 p. m., furled all sail but lower topsails and foretopmast staysail; 10 p. m., wind increasing to a strong gale, lay-to on the starboard tack, heading NNE., and sounded in 25 fathoms; midnight, blowing very hard, with heavy rain, barometer falling very fast; did not dare to reduce sail on account of the lee-shore. At 4.30 a. m. the wind shifted suddenly to NNE., blowing with hurricane force, with extreme cold and heavy snow, the vessel icing up very fast, and the barometer still falling; 5 a. m., tried to wear ship, the water shoaling rapidly, but the vessel ranged ahead on a course about WNW., on her beam ends, and would not mind the helm. At 5.30 cut the ropes of the lower main-topsail, and let it blow away. Tried again to wear ship under foretopsail and staysail, but again she refused her helm. Cut away the two remaining sails, to prevent her from ranging ahead toward the shore. At 10 a. m., yellow seas ahead, wind and sea driving the vessel toward the beach, crew paralyzed with wet and cold, when, at 10.30, the wind shifted suddenly to NNW., with increased violence and still colder weather. But the shift of wind had thrown the vessel's head off-shore, and, assisted by the helm, she came around and ran for the Gulf Stream, to get relief from the cold. Captain Grosse states that he has experienced many a tropical hurricane, but none of such long duration; it blew with hurricane force for twenty-four hours, and then a hard gale for a day and a half. The barometer ranged from 30.31 on the 10th to 29.21 the night of the 11th (exact time not noted). Relative to this low barometer reading, it would seem from other data to be fully .2 too low, unless the 12th be meant, and not the 11th.

Not far from the *Coryphene* was the American schooner *Phebe*, Captain Medero. In the afternoon it had been cloudy, with light rain, and a moderate breeze from ENE. to ESE. In the evening heavier rain, increasing easterly sea, falling barometer. Between 2 and 3 a. m., off Barnegat, in 8 fathoms of water, the wind went around to N., and in half an hour it was so cold that nothing could be done. Kept the vessel before the wind and ran out into the Gulf Stream. At 10 a. m. the wind was blowing almost a hurricane from NW., and the barometer, which had fallen to 29.10, remained the same throughout the day. March 13, still blowing a hurricane from WNW., very cold, with occasional squalls of snow; latter part, moderating, with rising barometer, but continuing squally, with occasional rain and snow, till the evening of the 15th.

On the afternoon of the 10th, the American schooner *Kensett*, Captain Smith, was about 100 miles E. from Cape Henry, bound N.; ESE. wind and fine weather. During the night the sky became overcast, and in the morning the sun rose red, and a long sea began to roll in from the east. At 10 a. m. picked up a pilot off Henlopen. In the afternoon it commenced raining, with falling barometer, but neither storm nor sea were very heavy. At 8 p. m. wore ship, wind blowing a double-reef breeze from east; Barnegat, by account, SW. 15 miles. The wind remained steady and did not increase till 3 a. m. of the 12th, when there was a heavy squall, but the wind did not shift. At 3.30 calm, so that the sails came amidships. At 4 o'clock the wind came from north with terrible force, blowing away all sail set; barometer 29.41. In an hour the vessel was covered with ice; 7 a. m., barometer 29.33. The wind continued NW. to WNW. throughout the day, the barometer rising slowly till 2 p. m., when it was 29.61, but after dark it fell again, reaching 29.41 again at 2 a. m., with wind NW., and 29.26 at 7 a. m. Wind NW. to WNW. during the 13th, with heavy cross seas. Squalls less frequent, dying away during the night of the 13th; 14th, nearly calm, with snow squalls. Continual snow during the 12th and 13th; thermometer 23°.

Ten miles SE. from Sandy Hook the American schooner *George Walker*, Captain Mitchell, reports the wind blowing with hurricane force from ESE. at midnight, corrected barometer reading 30.05 (this would seem to be fully .10 too high, indicating some error not accounted for). At 1 a. m. the wind shifted to E., barometer 29.85, and at 2 o'clock to NE., blowing a fresh gale with snow and very cold weather; 10 a. m., wind fully 60 miles per hour, barometer 29.55; 2 p. m., from 75 to 80 miles, 29.65. At 4 p. m. the wind was NNW., and on the 13th, 75 miles SE. from the Highlands, wind NW., barometer 29.45, clearing weather.

Also, about 35 miles SE¼E. from Sandy Hook, at midnight, the pilot-boat *Caprice*, Captain Sullivan, was in the central calm area which had just passed the coast; barometric pressure 29.80, decreasing rapidly. At 4 a. m. the wind came out suddenly from NNE., blowing a moderate gale, barometer 29.70. From 5 to 6 a. m. wind increasing in force, and finally blowing a hurricane from NNW., the barometer oscillating from 29.60 to 29.70, high cross sea from SE. and NE., fierce snow squalls and blinding spray. Lay-to under close reefed foresail and main-trysail, but had to take in the foresail, wind and sea were so high. The barometer fell to 29.50, and the vessel was boarded by combing seas which threw her on her beam ends. Lowest barometer 29.29, at noon on the 12th, oscillating until the gale moderated, the forenoon of the 13th.

We have now reviewed the whole line of coast from the Straits of Florida to Sandy Hook, and by means of various storm reports, selected from the large number at hand, have watched the effects of the great storm as it reached and passed the coast. These reports have clearly illustrated the general character of the storm, the phenomena attending the arrival and passage of the trough of low barometer, and its tremendous increase of energy upon reaching the coast. We may now go on to the consideration of the Weather Chart for 7 a. m., March 12, which illustrates more graphically than words can do the changes that the past twenty-four hours have seen developing.

CHAPTER V.

MARCH 12.

The chart shows the line, or trough, with isobars closely crowded together southward of Block Island, but still of a general elliptical shape, the lower portion of the line swinging eastward toward Bermuda, and carrying with it violent squalls of rain and hail far below the thirty-fifth parallel. The high land of Cuba and Santo Domingo prevented its effects from reaching the Caribbean Sea, although it was distinctly noticed on board the American bark *John J. Marsh*, Captain Whittier, southward of Cape Maysí, in the Windward Channel, where three hours of heavy rain were experienced during the day, with a shift of wind from SW. to NW. by N. The isotherm of 32° F. reaches from central Georgia to the coast below Norfolk, and thence out over the Atlantic to a point about 100 miles S. of Block Island, and thence due N., inshore of Cape Cod, explaining the fact that so little snow, comparatively, fell in Rhode Island and southeastern Massachusetts; from about Cape Ann it runs eastward to Cape Sable, and farther east it is carried southward again by the northeasterly winds off the Grand Banks. These northeasterly winds are part of the cyclonic system shown to the eastward of this and the preceding chart; farther south they become northerly and northwesterly, and it will be noticed that they have now carried the isotherm of 70° below the limits of the chart. Thus this chart shows very clearly the positions of warm and cold waves relative to such cyclonic systems; first, there is this cool wave in rear of the eastern cyclonic system, then a warm wave in front of the system advancing from the coast, and finally a cold wave of marked intensity following in its train.

By reference to the accompanying Track Chart and the storm reports published herewith the experience of any particular vessel can be referred to and studied in connection with each of these weather charts. Similarly, each wind-arrow on these charts represents a set of Greenwich noon observations, which can be referred to in the tables in the appendix by using as co-ordinates the date of the chart and the latitude and longitude of the center of the arrow. It will therefore be unnecessary to quote them in any great detail here, and only a few need be referred to.

Aboard the British steam-ship *Serapis*, Captain Dobson, the shift of wind took place very suddenly, in a heavy squall; there was no hauling or veering, and no calm intervened. This was between 5 and 6 a. m.; barometer at 6 o'clock, 29.7, falling .1 per hour; position, about latitude 39° 50′ N., longitude 73° W.; it had been blowing a heavy gale from ENE., overcast, misty and rainy. After the shift it blew with hurricane force from NW., accompanied by a heavy fall of snow, and the barometer continued to fall rapidly, not reaching its lowest point until 2 p. m., when it read 29.29 (position, about latitude 39° 30′ N., longitude 73° W.). Captain Dobson reports that at about 6 p. m. of the 11th, latitude 39° N., longitude 71° 40′ W., a bank of thick, black, inky clouds was seen to the SW.; it will be noticed, also, in the report from the British bark *Nora Wiggins*, that during the same afternoon, position about latitude 38° 30′ N., longitude 67° 30′ W., heavy, dark banks of clouds were seen both to the southward and northward; each of these vessels encountered the storm in great violence.

One of the very best reports is that received from Captain Urquhart, of the British steam-ship *Lord Clive*, westward-bound, whose position, when the trough reached him, was about latitude 39° N., longitude 71° 30′ W.; time, from 8.30 to 9 a. m. He states that at 8 o'clock the wind, which had been blowing a strong gale from ESE., moderated somewhat, with heavy rain; barometer 29.42.

At 8.30 the weather cleared up a little. At 9 the wind shifted suddenly to SW., blowing a whole gale, and at 9.30 to NW., blowing a complete hurricane, with violent squalls of hail and sleet. The barometer continued to fall (showing that the depression was still deepening), reaching the lowest point at 10 a. m., when its corrected reading was 29.18. This vessel's barometer was mercurial, compared with standard as soon as she reached Philadelphia, and as the central calm area passed directly over her this report gives reliable data by which to calculate the rate at which the depression was deepening. Assuming the reduced pressure at the center to have been 29.2, which is probably a trifle lower than it actually was, and that it was 28.9 at 10 p. m. (which we can safely do, as it was recorded as low as 28.92 at Wood's Holl, Mass.), we still have a decrease of pressure at the center of .30 inch in thirteen and one-half hours, or .18 in eight hours. This is almost as great a rate of decrease as was observed at times during the preceding twenty-four hours; thus the lowest recorded reading of the barometer at 7 a. m., the 11th, was 29.88 at Augusta, Ga.; at 3 p. m., 29.68 at Wilmington, N. C.; at 11 p. m., 29.35 on board the British steam-ship *Andes*, in the central calm area about 75 miles ENE. from Hatteras—an average rate of decrease of very nearly .23 in eight hours, and a maximum, from reliable observations, of .33.

These reports seem to indicate quite clearly that the secondary storm center that has formed off-shore, north of Hatteras, is becoming less elongated in shape and is developing enormous energy. The barometer diagram may well be studied in this connection, referring at the same time to the positions of signal stations and tracks of vessels plotted in red on the Track Chart. Although in several cases very low barometer readings have been reported, notably from the British bark *Nova Wingera* (28.57), the Norwegian bark *Wilhelm Birkedal* (28.64), and the American schooner *Messenger* (28.91), yet a careful consideration of all the data at hand indicates that these observations are not reliable. There can be little doubt that the lowest pressure occurred the night of the 12th, when the center was about Buzzard's Bay, or a little farther S., the corrected reading of the barometer at Wood's Holl, at 10 p. m., being 28.92; at Nantucket, 28.93; and at Block Island, 29. There happened to be no vessels at this time between Nantucket and Block Island, so far as our records show—fortunately for the vessels, no doubt, but unfortunately for the completeness of our meteorological data—and these readings must be considered about the lowest reliable readings recorded during the storm. At this time, too, the steepest barometric gradients are found, as indicated in the following table:

Maximum barometric gradients.

Station.	Barometer.	Range.	Distance in nautical miles.	Gradient.	
				Difference of pressure in [illegible] nautical miles.	Difference of pressure in [illegible] statute miles.
Block Island	[illegible]	[illegible]	0	[illegible]	[illegible]
New London	[illegible]	[illegible]	[illegible]	[illegible]	[illegible]
New Haven	[illegible]	[illegible]	[illegible]	[illegible]	[illegible]
New York	[illegible]	[illegible]	[illegible]	[illegible]	[illegible]
Albany	[illegible]	[illegible]	[illegible]	[illegible]	[illegible]

At 7 a. m. the following day very low readings are also reported: New Bedford, Mass., 28.91; Block Island, 28.92; and Wood's Holl, 28.96.

CHAPTER VI.

MARCH 13 AND 14.

The chart for 7 a. m., March 13, shows a marked decrease in the intensity of the storm, although the area over which stormy winds are blowing is still enormous, comprising, as it does, almost the entire region charted. From the Great Lakes and northern Vermont to the northern coast of Cuba the wind is blowing a gale from a direction almost invariably northwest, whilst westerly winds and low temperature have spread over a wide tract of ocean south of the fortieth parallel. North of this parallel the prevailing winds are easterly, the isobars extending in a general easterly and westerly direction. At the storm center off Block Island the pressure is 28.90, but the gradients are not so steep as on the preceding chart, and the severity of the storm, both ashore and at sea, has begun to diminish. About this center, too, the isobars are noticeably circular in form, showing that, although it first formed as an elliptical area, it gradually assumed the character of a true revolving storm, remaining almost stationary between Block Island and Nantucket until it had actually "blown itself out," while the great storm of which it was a conspicuous but not essential part was continuing its eastward progress. The enormous influx of cold air brought down by the long-continued northwesterly gale is graphically shown on this chart by the large extent and deepening intensity of the blue tint, where the temperatures are below the freezing point. From the northwestern to the southeastern portion of the chart we find a difference in temperature of more than 80° F. (from below −10° to above 70°), the steepest barometric pressure being found to the northwest of Block Island, where the pressure varies 1.80 inches in 750 miles (gradient, .036 inch in 15 nautical miles), and .66 inch in 126 miles (Block Island to Albany, N. Y.; gradient, .079).

On the chart for 7 a. m., March 14, the depression off Block Island has almost filled up, and the stormy winds have died out and become light and variable, with occasional snow squalls. The other storm center has now regained its ascendency, and is situated about 200 miles southeast from Sable Island, with a pressure about 29.3. The great wave of low barometer has overspread the entire western portion of the North Atlantic, with unsettled, squally weather from Labrador to the Windward Islands. The area of high pressure in advance has moved eastward, to be felt over the British Isles from the 17th to the 21st of the month, followed by a rapid fall of the barometer as this great atmospheric disturbance moves along its circuit round the northern hemisphere. The isotherm of 32° is still south of Hatteras, reaching well out off-shore, and thence northward, tangent to Cape Cod, as far as Central Maine, and thence eastward to St. John's, Newfoundland. Great contrasts of temperature and pressure are still indicated, but considerably less marked than on the preceding chart, and the normal conditions are being gradually restored.

It will be of interest briefly to refer here to a few reports selected from among the many which will be found printed in full in the appendix, in order to get a general idea of the character of the storm as it traversed the southward and eastward portions of the area charted. To the southward of Bermuda the Track Chart shows the tracks of the American bark *Wakefield*, Captain Crowell, and the German steam-ship *Catania*, Captain Franck. Captain Crowell's report shows that during the evening of the 12th it was clear and pleasant, wind freshening from SE. and S., sea smooth, barometer 30.02 at midnight (ship's time). During the forenoon of the 12th the wind increased rapidly from SW.; barometer 29.92. In the afternoon it clouded up, with passing showers, wind and sea increasing. From 4 p. m. to midnight, wind NW. and still increasing. At

8 p. m. the wind shifted suddenly to NNW. in a heavy squall of wind and rain; barometer 29.92. From midnight to 8 a. m. (14th), cloudy, with a strong breeze from W. by N.; sea rough, with a heavy swell. The barometer continued to fall till the evening of the 15th, when its corrected reading was 29.72; weather cloudy, with heavy squalls of wind and rain, blowing furiously from SW., the vessel laboring heavily and shipping large bodies of water. The weather did not moderate till the evening of the 16th.

The *Catania* was about 200 miles SW. by W. from Bermuda the morning of the 11th; barometer 30.22, fine weather, light breeze from ENE., dying out toward night. The afternoon of the 12th, strong gale from SSW. to W. and NW., with heavy rain during the night, followed by fine weather and moderate sea; lowest barometer 29.71, at 3 p. m. (75th meridian time); position, latitude 28° 20′ N., longitude 67° 50′ W. It will be noticed that the *Catania* was steaming to the SE., thus running out of the storm; the gale, as she experienced it, only lasted a few hours, with highest force of wind 10, and was followed by light variable winds and fine weather, with a high rolling sea from NNW.

To the northward and eastward of Bermuda the reports from the British ship *Glenburn*, Captain Johansen, and the British steam-ship *Caribbean*, Captain Daniel, may be mentioned. The *Glenburn* had encountered very heavy weather in the storm indicated to the eastward on the Weather Charts of March 11 and 12, and there was an interval of only one day between this storm and the succeeding one. The evening of the 12th there was a freshening southerly breeze, with cloudy, gloomy weather, vivid lightning all around the horizon, and occasional squalls. At 10 p. m. (ship's time) the wind shifted to the westward, with heavy rain, and increased to a fresh gale, with hard squalls; barometer 29.61. The weather continued unsettled and squally, with occasional rain and much thunder and lightning, for several days, the barometer rising slowly till the evening of the 14th, when it commenced to fall again, reaching its lowest point (29.47) the afternoon of the 15th.

The *Caribbean* was steaming in a direction about ENE., her position at noon of the 12th (ship's time) being latitude 34° 38′ N., longitude 63° 20′ W. She was overtaken by the storm on the 12th, the wind increasing to a gale from the SSE., ugly, threatening weather, with frequent squalls, accompanied by thunder and lightning. At about midnight it fell suddenly calm, barometer 29.30, and after a short interval the wind sprang up from the westward, increasing to a moderate gale, with squalls, passing showers, and a heavy cross sea.

To the northward the data are very complete, but it will answer for present purposes to refer to the report of the British steam-ship *Brooklyn City*, Captain Fitt, and the German ship *Anna*, Captain Menkens. The former was eastward-bound, along the transatlantic route, and during the forenoon of the 12th was heading into an increasing gale and heavy sea from ESE. At noon, latitude 40° 45′ N., longitude 65° 38′ W., squally, with heavy rain, wind ESE., 9, barometer 29.70. Wind and sea continued to increase, with falling barometer, till 11.30 p. m. (ship's time), when the wind shifted to W., with a high confused sea. The barometer continued to fall till 4 a. m. of the 13th, when its corrected reading was 29.36. The easterly winds were noticeably stronger than those from westward, due, at least in part, to the eastward motion of the vessel.

The *Anna* was farther eastward; her lowest barometer (29.57) was also experienced at 4 a. m. (ship's time), March 13, the wind blowing a strong gale from ESE.; position, latitude 41° 10′ N., longitude 54° 30′ W. Toward noon there were very heavy squalls of wind and rain, followed by an interval of calm at noon and then light southerly winds and six hours of heavy rain. During the evening heavy rain squalls, with thunder and lightning; and on the following day calms, variable winds, occasional heavy squalls, rain, thunder, and lightning. From the fact that the barometer commenced to rise several hours before the shift of wind, it is to be inferred that the depression was filling up and the energy of the storm decreasing. Still farther east, however, the depression deepened again, the result of the great contrasts of temperature and humidity always to be found off the Grand Banks, conditions that were intensified in the present case by the long-continued southerly and easterly winds that prevailed in advance of the storm, bringing up warm, moist air into contact with the cold Labrador current and the ice-fields in the Gulf of St. Lawrence. Captain Hughes, of the British steam-ship *Lord Gough*, for instance, reports a lowest corrected barometric pressure of 29.05, the afternoon of the 17th, latitude 48° 12′ N., longitude 35° 09′ W.; the gale set in on the 16th from S., coming up suddenly in a thick, black cloud, with torrents of rain and a high, confused sea. It blew with hurricane force for six hours, then fell calm for an hour, and blew with hurricane force for five hours more, the glass continuing to fall for some time after it had moderated; shifts of wind, S. to SSW. and WNW., then back to S. again. Other reports show that on the 17th, when the storm center was in about latitude 49° N., longitude 43° W., the reduced pressure was as low as 28.7.

The special feature of this great storm, or at least the feature that gave it such destructive violence ashore in the vicinity of New York, was the secondary storm center that remained so long about Block Island, moving about over a limited area, and gradually losing its identity as a distinct storm center. The following extract from the report made by Boat-keeper Robinson, in behalf of the pilots of New York pilot-boat No. 3 (the *Charles H. Marshall*), can not fail to be read with interest, giving, as it does, a very complete and continuous record of the weather a short distance off the coast, while the great "blizzard" was raging in New York. The gallant and successful struggle made by the crew of this little vessel for two long days and nights against such terrific odds is one of the most thrilling incidents of the storm, and well illustrates the dangers to which these hardy men are constantly exposed.

The *Charles H. Marshall* was off Barnegat the forenoon of the 11th, and as the weather looked threatening two more reefs were put in the sails and she was headed to the northward, intending to run into port for shelter. During the afternoon the breeze increased to a strong gale, and sail was reduced still further. When about 18 miles SE. from the light ship a dense fog shut in, and it was decided to remain outside and ride out the storm. The wind hauled to the eastward toward midnight, and at 3 a. m. it looked so threatening in the NW. that a fourth reef was taken in the mainsail and the foresail was treble reefed. In half an hour the wind died out completely, and the vessel lay in the trough of a heavy SE. sea that was threatening every moment to engulf her. She was then about 12 miles ESE. from Sandy Hook light ship, and in twenty minutes the gale struck her with such force from NW. that she was thrown on her beam ends. She instantly righted again, however, but in two hours was so covered with ice that she looked like a small iceberg. By 8 a. m. the wind had increased to a hurricane, the little vessel pitching and tossing in a terrific cross-sea, and only by the united efforts of the entire crew was it possible to partially lower and lash down the foresail and forestaysail. No one but those on board can realize the danger she was in from the huge breaking seas that rolled down upon her. The snow and rain came with such force that it was impossible to look to windward, and the vessel was lying broadside to wind and sea. A drag was rigged with a heavy log, anchor and hawser, to keep her head to sea and break the force of the waves, but it had little effect, and it was evident that something must be done to save the vessel. Three oil bags were made of duck, half filled with oakum saturated with oil, and hung over the side forward, amidships, and on the weather quarter. It is admitted that this is all that saved the boat and the lives of all on board, for the oil prevented the seas from breaking, and they swept past as heavy rolling swells. Another drag was rigged and launched, although not without great exertion and danger, and this helped a little. Heavy iron bolts had to be put in the oil bags to keep them in the water; and there the little vessel lay, fighting for life against the storm, refilling the oil bags every half hour, and fearing every instant that some passing vessel would run her down, as it was impossible to see a hundred feet in any direction. The boat looked like a wreck; she was covered with ice and it seemed impossible for her to remain afloat until daylight. Three oil bags were replenished every half hour during the night, all hands taking turn about to go on deck and fill them, crawling along the deck on hands and knees and secured with a rope in case of being washed overboard. Just before midnight a heavy sea struck the boat and sent her over on her side; everything movable was thrown to leeward, and the water rushed down the forward hatch. But again she righted, and the fight went on. The morning of the 13th it was still blowing with hurricane force, the wind shrieking past in terrific squalls. It cleared up a little toward evening, and she wore around to head to the northward and eastward, but not without having her deck swept by a heavy sea. It moderated and cleared up the next day, and after five hours of hard work the vessel was cleared of ice and sail set for home. She had been driven 100 miles before the storm, fighting every inch of the way, her crew without a chance to sleep, frost-bitten, clothes drenched and no dry ones to put on, food and fuel giving out, but they brought her into port without the loss of a spar or sail, and she took her station on the bar as usual.

Do the pages of history contain the record of a more gallant fight? Nothing could show more graphically than this brief report the violence and long duration of the storm. No wonder that this terrific northwest gale drove the ocean itself before it, so that the very tides did not resume their normal heights for nearly a week at certain ports along the coast, and the Gulf Stream itself was far south of its usual limits. The damage and destruction wrought ashore are too fresh in mind to be referred to here, and losses along the coast can only be mentioned briefly. Below Hatteras there was little damage done to shipping. In Chesapeake Bay 2 barks, 77 schooners, and 17 sloops were blown ashore, sunk, or damaged; in Delaware Bay, 37 vessels; along the New Jersey coast and in the Horseshoe at Sandy Hook, 13; in New York Harbor and along the Long Island coast, 20; and along the New England coast, 9. The names of six vessels that were abandoned at sea have been reported, and there are at least nine others missing, among them the lamented New York pilot-boats *Phantom* and *Enchantress* and the yacht *Cythera*; moreover, shortly after the storm seven derelicts, which can not be identified with any previously reported, were sighted off the coast, to take their places amongst the other obstructions to navigation whose positions and erratic tracks are plotted each month on the Pilot Chart, that other vessels may be warned of the danger of collision. The abandoned schooner *W. L. White* has started off to the eastward in the Gulf Stream, and will soon become a source of anxiety to the captains of steam ships along the transatlantic route, and furnish a brief sensation to the passengers when she is sighted. There is thus an intensely human side to the history of a great ocean storm, and to one who reads these brief records of facts and at the same time gives some little play to his imagination there is a very pathetic side to the picture—a side that is only too often "out of sight, out of mind" to the great majority who live ashore, and to whom the slowly accumulating evidences of a great storm at sea, with its fragmentary and always incomplete record of disasters, sometimes seem, in this age of the electric telegraph, like pages of ancient history.

CHAPTER VII.

THE USE OF OIL TO PREVENT HEAVY SEAS FROM BREAKING.

The following reports are selected from those received relative to the use of oil by vessels caught in the heavy cross-seas of this great storm. In accordance with the policy followed hitherto by the Hydrographic Office, which has already resulted in the almost universal recognition of the practical benefits to be derived from the use of oil at sea to quiet dangerous waves, these reports will be quoted verbatim. The object has been, and is now, to call attention as widely as possible to this subject; to publish facts, actual experiences, with dates, positions, names, and all details that may tend to bring it vividly and graphically before every navigator, that each one may see for himself what others think of it, how they have tried the experiment, and the results gained. In this way it is shown very clearly that very little trouble and expense are involved; that almost any kind of oil may be used to advantage; and that underwriters, owners, agents, and masters, all over the world, have become thoroughly convinced that the recent revival of the knowledge and use of this old but almost forgotten principle is a matter of the greatest importance to them all. Many vessels are now fitted out with special apparatus for distributing oil most advantageously; numerous patents have been taken out for special kinds of oil and special methods of distribution; but the most important fact of all is brought out by each and every one of the following reports, namely, that every vessel has on board at all times materials which, by means of a little ingenuity and care, will answer the purpose, and which may, by such use, avert not only discomfort and damage, but even serious disaster.

From some of these vessels separate storm reports have been received, which have been referred to already in this discussion. Others, however, are new, and in addition to the special information relative to the use of oil will be found to contain interesting data about the storm itself.

Several of the New York pilot boats used oil to advantage, and their hazardous occupation would seem to make a knowledge of its use on such occasions of the greatest value. Captain Sullivan, of the *Caprice*, for instance, whose interesting storm report has been quoted above, states that when he was boarded by combing seas off Sandy Hook, which threw his vessel on her beam ends, he broke out oil-bags, stuffed them with oakum, rags, and anything he could lay his hands on, poured in a mixture of 1 gallon lard oil, 1 gallon paint oil, and 3 gallons petroleum (all he had on board), and punched them with a brad-awl. One of these he hung over the weather bow and the other over the side, abreast the weather-main rigging, so as to just clear the water when on an even keel; he also rigged out two drags over the weather-bow, each composed of 15 fathoms of chain on five fenders, held by 75 fathoms of hawser. After the oil was used no water came on board, although before using it the sea was making a clean breach over the vessel. A breaking wave would rush toward her, meet the oil slick, the crest would quiet down, and the wave roll harmlessly past. He used the oil for thirty-six hours, and says it saved his vessel.

The pilot-boat *Charles H. Marshall* was struck by the storm at 10.30 p. m. on the 11th, 10 miles E. from Sandy Hook, wind WNW., with snow. A brief report from Pilot Partridge states that the vessel drifted 100 miles before the gale, till she was brought head to wind the morning of the 13th, with anchor and 90 fathoms of chain which held for 24 hours, the wind blowing 100 miles per hour. Used three oil-bags, and except for them he thinks the vessel would have gone down. The detailed report of Boat-keeper Robinson, printed in full elsewhere, can not fail to be read with the greatest interest. The account of the use of oil is such an essential part of the report that it is quoted entire therewith. Similarly with regard to the pilot boat *William H. Starbuck*, off Barnegat, the night of March 11. The report communicated by Pilot Heath, printed in full elsewhere, may be referred to in this connection, and no stronger testimony regarding the advantages to be derived from the use of oil could be desired than the brief but eloquent facts stated in these two reports.

The experience of the yacht *Iroquois*, off Henlopen, has been spoken of already, but the special feature of the report received from her sailing-master, Captain Norton, is that relating to the use of oil. At 1 a. m., the 12th, when it was blowing a most terrific gale, he found the vessel was making too much headway for safety; took in the reefed fore-stay-sail and fore-try-sail, and put over a patent sea-drag, but the hawser carried away and he lost it. He then thought of a case of oil on board, containing four 5-gallon cans; made three bags of No. 5 cotton, large enough to hold about 2 gallons apiece; put 2 quarts in each, and hung them over the weather-bow, but the oil congealed and would not run out through the holes he had made with a sail-needle. Then tried the oil through the pipes of the closet in the forecastle, near the bow, putting a few table-spoonfuls in the bowl and then pumping it out. It was truly wonderful to see the effect it had on the sea. A huge comber would come down upon the vessel, threatening to bury her 20 feet deep. The comb would strike a patch of oil no larger than a common dining table, and in an instant the top of the sea was smooth and round, without even a wind ripple, and the little schooner would pop up on top of it as easy as a gull. He stood on the deck for more than an hour watching the effect, and then went below feeling that so far as breaking waves were concerned he was perfectly safe as long as the oil held out. The oil used in this case was a soft, greasy oil, which he thinks is the best. The yacht rode out the storm in perfect safety, without any damage, although both top-masts were on end and jib boom out. Used 15 gallons of oil in thirty-six hours. Captain Norton has followed the sea for the past thirty years, seventeen of them as master, but never experienced a worse gale than this.

Captain Trim, of the American schooner *Isaac Orbeton*, was caught in the hurricane off Absecom; fore-sail blown away; sea very high and irregular; rain, sleet, and snow; wind from WNW. The vessel was heavily laden with sugar, and Captain Trim hove-to and prepared to use oil to prevent the sea from breaking over her. Rigged six oil-bags as follows: from the weather cat-head, from each weather-chains, on the boat davits, and on a buoy to windward (a heavy piece of timber secured to the vessel by a lanyard); filled the bags with oakum, pricking the canvas well with a sail-needle, and used equal parts of fish-oil and kerosene, refilling the bags about every two hours. No water came on board during the thirty hours the oil was used. The vessel was very deep and must otherwise have been greatly damaged by the heavy seas, which, though very high and irregular, were reduced by the oil to long rolling swells. He never tried the experiment before, but regards the use of oil as a most valuable thing, if the bags are attended to and not allowed to get empty. Used about 10 gallons each of fish oil and kerosene.

The American schooner *John H. Kranz*, Captain Pitcher, was at anchor off Brandywine Shoal, Delaware Bay, at the beginning of the storm; her chains parted and she was driven to sea, scudding under bare poles. Captain Pitcher reports that heavy seas broke on board, smashed his booms, and made it unsafe to move about the deck. He immediately set to work to use oil, placing a can in the after closet in such a way as to allow the oil to drip slowly out. He also poured oil on deck, from forward aft. The effect was wonderful; no more water came on board, and the vessel ran before the hurricane in perfect safety. He considers fish oil best, and intends never to go to sea without a supply.

Captain Cottrell, American schooner *[illegible]*, was struck by the hurricane off Five Fathom Bank at 1.30 a. m., March 12; snowing, and bitterly cold; dangerously heavy and irregular sea. At 2 a. m. he squared away and ran for the Gulf Stream under bare poles, having placed an oil-bag in each mizzen chains; the bags were filled with oakum and fish oil, and perforated with a sail-needle. There was a tremendous following sea, and, finding that the waves broke over the vessel amidships, he carried the bags forward, one on each jib-boom guy, after which he ran with perfect safety and comfort, so far as taking water was concerned. He continued to use oil for fifty-two hours, and the high following seas were reduced to harmless swells as they struck the slick. Two attempts were made to bring the vessel by the wind, but it proved to be too dangerous until the Gulf Stream was reached and some sail could be made. Captain Cortrall states that the magical effect of the oil is absolutely incredible until one sees the experiment tried, and he will never go to sea again without being in readiness to use it.

Captain Segerman, American bark *Serene*, was hove-to off the Chesapeake from the 11th to the 15th of March, and used oil with marked effect to prevent seas from breaking on board. Canvas bags were hung from each weather-channel, containing a little oakum and about a quart of oil each. Only 4 gallons of linseed-oil were used during the gale, which lasted three days.

Captain Andrews, American schooner *Warren B. Potter*, was to the eastward of Cape Henry and ran to the southeast before the storm. As the vessel was shipping a great deal of water, and the seas very high and irregular, he prepared to use oil. Took a sheet off a bed and dipped it in paint-oil, put it in a bag and towed it astern. Then hung bags on each side of fore-channels, filled with rags and oil. The result was that the waves no longer broke over the vessel. He has tried kerosene, but can not advise using it.

The American schooner *Normandy*, also to the eastward of Cape Henry, was in the hurricane for three days, and lost main-gaff, mainsail and foresail, and split the jib. The long-boat and one davit were carried away, companion-way doors and window-shutters broken, binnacle washed away, cabin flooded, and main deck swept of everything movable. Further damage was avoided by simply pouring oil over the side.

The American schooner *Ellen M. Golder*, Captain Johnston, encountered the storm off the coast of Long Island. The vessel was hove-to, but as the wind and sea increased it became necessary to wear ship and scud before the gale. A tremendous sea was running and the vessel was under bare poles, all sail having been blown away. In order to perform the maneuver in safety the captain decided to try the use of oil; poured 5 gallons of paint-oil over the lee-quarter, and the vessel wore around without taking a drop of water on board, although the captain feels sure that without the use of oil it would have been wholly impossible.

Captain Saint John, American schooner *Spartan*, was struck by the gale off Montauk Point, March 11, and blown 200 miles off shore, losing all of his sails and much of his standing rigging. While running before the gale, with a prospect of foundering in the heavy sea, the captain threw overboard a number of oil-soaked bags of oakum. The waves, however, washed the bags back on deck as fast as they were thrown over. The captain finally poured a quantity of oil through the closet pipe and secured comparatively calm water, saving his vessel.

Storm reports are quoted elsewhere from the British bark *Nora Wiggins*, the German bark *Johanna*, the American schooner *Messenger*, and the American ship *Annie M. Small*. From each of these a report has been received regarding the use of oil in the great storm, and in every case its use was regarded as of great advantage.

Mr. Collins, mate of the *Nora Wiggins*, states that, when hove-to in the hurricane, the vessel was boarded by breaking seas. Oil bags were used with great effect to prevent the combing waves from breaking over the vessel, and oil was also poured on oakum put in the bowls of the closet, and allowed to run slowly out the pipes. The bags were made fast to the main rigging just clear of the water, and kept the sea smooth. No water came on board after the oil was used.

Captain Falker, of the *Messenger*, made use of oil for the first time in this storm; he was thoroughly converted, and is now a firm believer in the great advantages to be gained. Not having any regular appliances, he put a can of porpoise-oil, with a small hole in the bottom for the oil to drip through, in the after closet, thus allowing the oil to drip slowly into the sea. The result was astonishing. The oil cut the combers completely from the running seas and made the water so smooth about the vessel that little or no water came on board. The vessel was hove-to for fifty-two hours, and only five gallons of oil expended.

Finally, Captain Meyer, of the *Johanna*, when he found it necessary to abandon his vessel, in a sinking condition, was lying-to on the starboard tack, a strong northwest gale blowing, the seas running very high and breaking. The German bark *Weser* ran down to leeward and hove-to. Got two boats ready, hove two cans of rape seed oil over to windward, punctured so that the oil could run out, and manned the boats, each of which was supplied with fish-oil, in cans. Pulled under the lee of the *Johanna* to the *Weser*, all the time pouring oil over the stern of the boats. The boats were half full of water when they got alongside the *Weser*, but he thinks they would never have reached her had they not used oil.

Such reports need little or no comment. The mere publication of the facts is enough to convince any one. With the memory fresh in mind of the loss of the gallant New York pilot boats *Phantom* and *Enchantress*, of the lamented yacht *Cythera*, and other vessels, some of them not yet given up but probably lost in this terrific storm, these brief reports convey a lesson which can not fail to be heeded and remembered.

CHAPTER VIII.

CONCLUSION.

The great storm that has thus been briefly described, as well as can be done from the data now at hand and in the limited time at our disposal, would seem to deserve more notice than a mere sensation over its fierce onslaught and destructive progress. This study can not be brought to a conclusion more fittingly than by pointing out certain things which it has emphasized, certain lessons which it has taught, that we may learn from the lesson of experience to-day how best to shape our course to-morrow.

First of all, it has furnished a most striking and instructive example of a somewhat unusual class of storms, and this on such a grand scale, and in a part of the world where the data for its study are so complete, that it must long remain a most memorable instance. It is a case where the law of storms, founded on the circular theory and the eight point rule, is to a large extent inapplicable as a guide for action; because here, instead of a more or less circular area of low barometer at the storm center, there is a great trough of "low" between two ridges of "high," the whole system moving rapidly eastward, and including, "within the arc of its majestic sweep," almost the entire width of the temperate zone. Relative to the law of storms, however, this much may be said with perfect safety: no storm, however abnormal its character, is going to lessen confidence in general rules derived from experience in thousands of storms and in every ocean. The "trough phenomena," as an eminent meteorologist has called the violent squalls, with shifts of wind and change of conditions generally at about the time of lowest barometer, are to be expected and guarded against in every storm, and sailors have long ago summed them up, to store away in memory for practical use when occasion demands, in the well known lines—

First rise after low
Indicates a stronger blow.

These lines do not, of course, take into consideration the fact that if the depression of the storm center is deepening, or, as we may say, the energy of the storm increasing, the violent shift of wind and "stronger blow" will be experienced before the time of lowest barometer, an occurrence very frequently illustrated during the storm now under consideration. On the other hand, if the storm is decreasing in violence, the change may occur some time after the barometer has begun to rise. There are many similar verses that are well known among sailors, and while most of them may seem very crude and some of them involve rules of action that can not be recommended, yet on the whole they serve a very useful purpose, and are often remembered and acted upon long after more elaborate rules have been forgotten.

It has called attention anew to the sudden deepening of depressions upon reaching the coast, and the corresponding increase of energy to be expected, a lesson that should be borne in mind by every navigator leaving port with a falling barometer and other signs of a storm. It has reminded us of the vitally important influence of the Gulf Stream in causing such increase of energy, and to the necessity of closely watching this great warm ocean-current and noting any abnormal conditions of volume, velocity, temperature, or position; especially so during the spring and autumn months, the periods of most rapid change in the conditions of oceanic and atmospheric circulation. The accompanying Barometer Diagram, if studied in connection with the Track Chart and the Weather Chart for March 11, illustrates very clearly this deepening of the depression at the storm center. It may be said in this connection, however, that it would seem wholly impossible to have foretold the formation and persistency off Block Island of a secondary storm center of such energy as was developed in this case, so far as our present knowledge is concerned, and a prediction to that effect made under similar circumstances would probably prove wrong in at least nine cases out of ten.

It has enforced in most unmistakable terms the importance, not only to our extensive shipping interests but to the people of all our great sea-board cities, of the establishment of telegraphic signal stations at outlying points off the coast: at St. Johns (or Cape Race) and Sable Island, to watch the movement of areas of high barometer, upon which that of the succeeding "low" so largely depends; and at Bermuda, Nassau, and various points in the West Indies and Windward Islands, that we may be forewarned of the approach and progress of the terrific hurricanes which, summer after summer, bring devastation and destruction along our Gulf and Atlantic coasts, and of whose fury this great storm is an approximate example and a timely reminder. Moreover, there are other important objects to be gained, in addition to the better forecasting of stormy weather off our coasts and along the transatlantic routes. Every edition of the Pilot Chart records the latest reported position of numerous derelict vessels and other dangers to navigation—submerged wrecks, buoys adrift, icebergs, and masses of field ice. But at present such reports are necessarily several days old, and the present positions of these dangerous obstructions must be roughly estimated, allowing for their probable drift in the interval of time that has elapsed since the report was made. There are recorded, also, the probable limits of frequent fog for the ensuing month and the regions where fog was most frequently reported during the preceding month. But general averages only give the regions where fog is most likely to be encountered; they do not and can not attempt to state whether or no there will be a fog at a given place at a given time. But scientific research and practical inventive genius, advancing hand in hand for the benefit of mankind, have discovered not only the laws governing the formation of the dense banks of fog that have made the Grand Banks dreaded by navigators, but also the means by which certain facts may be observed, telegraphed, charted, and studied a thousand miles away, and the occurrence of fog predicted with almost unfailing accuracy, even whilst the very elements themselves are only preparing for its formation. By means of such predictions the safety of navigation along the greatest highway of ocean traffic in the world would be vastly increased—routes traversed yearly at almost railway speed by vessels intrusted with more than a million human lives and property of an aggregate value of fully a billion dollars.

To masters of vessels of every nationality whose voluntary and cordial co-operation have alone rendered it possible to write this history with any completeness, it is hoped that this brief discussion will emphasize the importance of accurately and carefully taking and recording meteorological observations, both at frequent intervals during stormy weather, when the conditions are changing rapidly, and at stated times during fair weather as well. The character and progress of a storm are not isolated phenomena which can be considered and discussed from a knowledge of the conditions that hold good over a limited area; on the contrary, to be thoroughly understood there must be at hand a large number of reliable observations, taken with instruments whose errors are known by means of a recent comparison with standard, and from vessels at various points over a wide tract of ocean. The importance of the simultaneous observations is illustrated by the accompanying charts, based almost entirely upon them. By means of such data the isobars and isotherms of the continents, plotted on the daily international chart by means of data taken at land stations in every civilized country of the globe, can be extended across the intervening oceans, forming on one sheet an instantaneous photograph, as it were, of the meteorological conditions of an entire hemisphere.

Finally, it may be safely said that nothing will more forcibly attract the attention of the practical navigator than the new and striking illustrations which have been furnished by reports from various masters of vessels caught in the terrific winds and violent cross seas of this great storm, relative to the use of oil to prevent heavy broken seas from coming on board. Nor can anything be more gratifying to this Office than to receive constantly such conclusive proof that its efforts to force this subject upon the attention of navigators by means of the Pilot Chart and various other publications have resulted in such a notable decrease in the unavoidable dangers of the sea.

APPENDIX.

MISCELLANEOUS METEOROLOGICAL DATA.
WRECKAGE ALONG THE COAST.
DETAILED STORM REPORTS.
GREENWICH NOON OBSERVATIONS.

MISCELLANEOUS METEROLOGICAL DATA.

TOTAL WIND MOVEMENT, MARCH 11-14.

The following figures are selected from data published by the U. S. Signal Service:

	Miles.		Miles.
Block Island, R. I	2,392	Hatteras, N. C	2,296
Philadelphia, Pa	2,552	Boston, Mass	2,212
Eastport, Me	2,529	Norfolk, Va	2,301
Atlantic City, N. J	2,526	New York, N. Y	2,180

SNOW AND RAIN FALL IN SOUTHERN NEW ENGLAND, MARCH 11-14.

Prof. Winslow Upton, secretary to the New England Meteorological Society, says (American Meteorological Journal, May, 1888):

In the region embracing nearly the southern half of Vermont and of New Hampshire west of the Merrimac, the western half of Massachusetts, nearly the whole of Connecticut and of New York east of the Hudson as far north as Lake George, the average depth of unmelted snow exceeded 30 inches, while in central Connecticut and a large part of eastern New York the average fall was over 40 inches. Within this area there seems to have been a region near the Connecticut River in Massachusetts where the fall was a little less than 30 inches, and a more marked region in the vicinity of Hartford, Conn., where the fall was less than 20 inches. In Rhode Island and eastern Massachusetts, where the precipitation was snow and rain mixed, the amount of rain was excessive. Some of the snow-drifts actually measured were of astonishing height. In Bangall, Dutchess County, N. Y., the measurements gave heights from 15 to 40 feet, and in Cheshire, New Haven County, Conn., one of 38 feet was measured. The maximum precipitation reported was at Middletown, Conn., 5.78 inches.

The detailed chart of isobars and isotherms for 10 p. m., March 12, accompanying Professor Upton's paper, shows a difference of temperature of 25° in 75 miles (from southeastern Massachusetts to central Connecticut).

The precipitation mentioned above may be considered heavy, although by no means remarkable. Had it not been for the fact that in the vicinity of New York it was almost wholly in the form of snow, causing great obstruction to traffic and almost entire suspension of business, it would not have attracted such great attention. The heaviest rain-falls probably occur in India; in northern Bengal, for instance, a daily average of 12.1 inches of rain fell from May 28 to June 3, 1887, and at Dewangunj, district of Mymensingh, 19.67 inches in one day (June 1, 1887), equal to 1,600,000 tons of water per square mile. At Cherrapungi, Assam, about 300 miles NE. from Calcutta, the *average annual rainfall* is 493 inches, of which 325 inches fell in June, July and August; in one year (1861) 905 inches fell, in one month (August, 1841), 264 inches, and in one day (June 14, 1876), 41 inches.

WATERSPOUTS REPORTED DURING THE STORM.

Captain Brunn, Norwegian steam-ship *Faedrelandet*, observed a number of small waterspouts, probably twenty or thirty, March 14, between 4 and 8 a. m. (ship's time), latitude 34° 50' N., longitude 74° 41' W., to latitude 35° 3' N., longitude 74° 41' W. They were traveling with the wind, which was blowing a heavy gale from NNW., and rotating in a direction opposite to the motion of the hands of a watch. The weather was threatening and stormy looking, with very wet fog. Temperature of the air 46°; water 72°. Barometer 29.72 (corrected). This report is especially interesting when considered in connection with the following report, received from Captain Bermpohl, British steam-ship *Samana*, who was about 60 miles to leeward of the *Faedrelandet*, and who reports that on March 14, latitude 34° 10′ N., longitude 74° 16′ W., he observed many waterspouts between 8 a. m. and noon. It will be noticed that both vessels were in the southwest quadrant of the storm; a cold northwesterly gale was blowing over the warm Gulf Stream current, and the waterspouts sighted by Captain Brunn near the western edge of the stream were evidently associated with those sighted a few hours later by Captain Bermpohl, 60 miles to leeward. An excellent detailed report made out by First Officer O'Brien, of the *Samana*, gives many interesting particulars regarding the spouts sighted from that vessel. They were of different sizes, all ascending with a spiral motion to the clouds and then disappearing. One came within about a mile of the ship, and they were all within from one to three miles. They appeared to rotate in a direction against the hands of a watch, and were traveling in a southerly direction. There was a strong gale from west, hauling to northwest, with occasional snow, and a blinding spray flying over the vessel. Clouds, cirro-cumulus and stratus. Temperature of water 74°.

A FEW GULF STREAM REPORTS.

From among the many reports at hand relative to the Gulf Stream, the following may be quoted as being of special interest in this connection.

Captain Freeman, American steam-ship *Hudson*, at New York, February 28, from New Orleans, reports that he encountered an unusually strong current in the straits of Florida, strongest between Fowey Rocks and Jupiter. Passed Fowey Rocks at a distance of about 9 miles, Jupiter Inlet, 12 miles; there was a light SSE. wind, and it had been blowing from that direction for several days. From Sombrero to Alligator had a 4 knot current, and it continued strong as far north as latitude 31° N., when it slowed down, running about 2 knots with the ship, from latitude 31° N. to latitude 34° N., on a course about NE., near the western edge of the stream. The temperature of the surface water was as follows, at noon, Greenwich mean time, each day:

Date.	Lat. N.	Long. W.	Temperature.
Feb. 24 ...	24 .20′	80 .05′	77°
Feb. 25 ...	29 .08	79 .47	78
Feb. 26 ...	33 .34	76 .43	72
Feb. 27 ...	37 .24	74 .36	68

The above is a fair sample of reports, showing that the current was unusually strong toward the end of February; during the first ten days of March the prevailing winds were southeasterly and southerly, still further increasing its volume, velocity, and temperature.

The reports that are quoted below are merely isolated reports, indicating in a very general way the effect upon the Gulf Stream of the long-continued northwest gale.

Captain Philbrook, American schooner *Fostino*, reports that at noon, March 13, his position was latitude 26° 10′ N., longitude 79° 49′ W. The wind was then NNW., force 8, and the sea heavier than he had ever seen it in the Gulf Stream. To the northward of the thirtieth parallel he could detect no current whatever.

Captain Daniel, British steam-ship *Caribbean*, states that on March 14, at 6 p. m. (ship's time), latitude 37° 50′ N., longitude 54° 53′ W., he encountered a strong race of current, with a strong current ripple at times; temperature of water, 65°. A current ripple was also noticed on the 16th, latitude 40° 27′ N., longitude 47° 1′ W.

Captain Cates, American brig *Arcot*, reports that on March 16 he found a band of warm Gulf current, temperature 75°, latitude 35° 2′ N., longitude 70° 5′ W., to latitude 35° 30′ N., longitude 71° 35′ W., setting to the *southwestward*, with a band of cold water (temperature 45°) between it and the main stream, which seemed to be some 60 miles to the southeast of its usual position.

Captain Barstow, American bark *James S. Stone*, reports as follows: March 19, latitude 36° 12′ N., longitude 75° 17′ W., crossed the inner edge of the Gulf Stream, which was very clearly defined as far as the eye could reach. The current itself, running about ENE., could be easily distinguished, flowing past the colder wall of water along its western boundary. The wind at the time was very light and the sea smooth.

BAROMETER OSCILLATIONS.

Remarkable fluctuations of the barometer are reported as follows:

American schooner *Nantasket*, about 70 miles E. from Cape Henry. Lowest barometer, 29.50, at 10 p. m., March 11. For the first twelve hours, and in fact for nearly twenty-four hours, the barometer vibrated in the most remarkable way, as much as .15 inch at a time.

New York pilot boat *Caprice*, off Sandy Hook. From 5 to 6 a. m., March 12, the barometer oscillated between 29.60 and 29.70.

New York pilot-boat *Edward E. Barrett*; position at noon, March 13, latitude 40° 23′ N., longitude 70° 15′ W. Barometer 29.21 at 4 a. m., oscillating from 29.16 to 29.26.

American schooner *Ellen M. Golder*, about 30 miles S. from Shinnecock, Long Island. March 12, 2 p. m., barometer vibrating between 29.09 and 29.07.

ELECTRIC PHENOMENA.

The following table has been prepared, for convenience of reference, of reports of electric phenomena. The original reports may be consulted for additional and more detailed information.

Vessel.	Date.	Approximate position.
[illegible]	Mar. 11	Latitude [illegible] N., longitude [illegible] W.
[illegible]	do	Latitude [illegible] N., longitude [illegible] W.
Melissa Trask	do	Off Hatteras.
[illegible]	do	Latitude [illegible] N., longitude [illegible] W.
[illegible]	do	Latitude [illegible] N., longitude [illegible] W.
Warren B. Potter	do	Off Hatteras.
[illegible]	Mar. 12	Latitude [illegible] N., longitude [illegible] W.
[illegible]	do	Latitude [illegible] N., longitude [illegible] W.
[illegible]	do	Latitude [illegible] N., longitude [illegible] W.
[illegible]	do	Latitude [illegible] N., longitude [illegible] W.
[illegible]	Mar. 13	Latitude [illegible] N., longitude [illegible] W.
[illegible]	Mar. 14	Latitude [illegible] N., longitude [illegible] W.
[illegible]	do	Latitude [illegible] N., longitude [illegible] W.
[illegible]	Mar. 15	Latitude [illegible] N., longitude [illegible] W.

EXTRACT FROM THE CANADIAN MONTHLY WEATHER REVIEW.

The following extract from the Monthly Weather Review for March, published by the meteorological service of the Dominion of Canada, Prof. Charles Carpmael, director, will be found of interest in connection with the history of the great storm:

Until the morning of the 8th the pressure in the northwest had been generally of an anti-cyclonic nature, with continued cold fine weather. A depression, however, which had apparently moved in from the Pacific, had crossed the Rocky Mountains on the 7th, and its northern limits, which then extended over the northwest, caused a snowfall throughout the Territories, and for a short time a little milder weather in Manitoba, which, however, was succeeded again on the 9th by higher pressure and more cold weather.

On the night of the 9th the reports showed a new developing anti-cyclone over the whole northwest and western States and Territories; the earlier anti-cyclone which had hovered in the northwest, now central over Quebec, and the cyclonic system from the Pacific as an elongated trough of low pressure stretching from Lake Superior to Texas.

During the 10th a slow easterly progression of these systems took place. The wind increased in the Lake District from the E. and S., and higher temperature and rain became general. Next day this movement continued, the anti-cyclones keeping their relative positions, and the cyclonic trough now showing as two distinct but small depressions, one of which was by night disappearing over Quebec, whilst the other was increasing in energy over the Middle Atlantic coast, and snow had extended with higher temperatures to Quebec.

At 7 a. m. on the 12th the northern depression had disappeared, the two anti-cyclones had apparently joined forces over eastern Canada, and the southern cyclone was developing in energy, accompanied by a heavy snowfall in the New England States. By the 13th it had developed into a severe storm; a gale of wind extended throughout the Lake and eastern districts, accompanied by snow in Ontario, Quebec, and New Brunswick, and rain in Nova Scotia, heavy drifts seriously impeding railway traffic. The cyclone continued to hover over or near the New England coast and gradually dispersed there, causing a continuance of high winds in Quebec and the maritime provinces till the night of the 14th, by which time high pressure had spread over the country with fairer weather, accompanied by decidedly low temperatures in Ontario, and continued moderate temperatures in the eastern provinces.

BAHAMA ISLANDS.

Commander Ed. Scobell Clapp, R. N., inspector of imperial light-houses, Nassau, N. P., has forwarded a very complete detailed report of observations made on board the light-house tender *Richmond*, March 10–15. The report came to hand too late to be used in the preparation of this monograph, but the following extracts are published as of special interest in this conection:

Date.	Time.	Wind.	Barometer.	Thermometer	Weather.	Remarks.
				°		
Mar. 11	Noon	S. by E. 6	29.964	72	o. m.	At anchor 1½ miles WNW. from Elbow Cay light, Abaco.
Mar. 12	4 a. m.	N. 7	29.894	68	o. g.	7 a. m., wind shifted from SW. to NNW.; 7.30 a.m., bar. 29.864.
	6 a. m.	N. 7	29.966	69	o. g.	
Mar. 13	Noon	WNW. 6	30.027	69	b. c. m.	1 p. m., passed out through Man of War Channel.
	4 p. m.	W. 7	29.997	69	b. c. m.	
Mar. 14	8 a. m.	NW. 5	30.039	69	b. c.	7 a. m., off Nassau; bar breaking, danger flag hoisted at light-house.

BERMUDA.

The following extracts are quoted from the weekly report of the weather at Gibbs' Hill Light Station, Bermuda, published in the Bermuda Royal Gazette; observations made by Josephus Perinchief, at noon, local mean time.

Date.	Wind.		Barometer.	Thermometer	Remarks.
				°	
Mar. 11	NW.	4	29.97	58	Fine.
Mar. 12	S.	7	29.55	58	Thick, rainy.
Mar. 13	WNW.	4	29.61	56	Unsettled, squalls.
Mar. 14	SW.	5	29.50	57	Do.
Mar. 15	W. to NW.	7	29.49	55	Hail, squalls, and rain.
Mar. 16	NW.	6	29.81	59	Fine, cloudy.

WRECKAGE ALONG THE COAST.

NOTE.—This list has been carefully revised from the latest and best data at hand.

NEW ENGLAND.

Along the New England coast 15 schooners and 1 tug were damaged, the names of which follow:

Schooner Ida E. Latham,
Schooner Cordova,
Schooner Daniel,
Schooner A. C. Parker,
Schooner Lulu,
Schooner Ella,
Schooner Norma,
Schooner John Somers,
Schooner Dreadnaught,
Schooner Emma Jane,
Schooner Lizzie Hayes,
Schooner M. B. Linscott,
Schooner S. A. Parkhurst,
Schooner Wanderer,
Schooner Maggie Bruce,
Tug Deo Volente.

NEW YORK AND LONG ISLAND.

Of the vessels in and about New York and near the Long Island shores, 2 barks, 6 schooners, 3 tug-boats (one with a tow), 5 pilot-boats, 2 lighters, 1 ferry-boat, 1 barge, 2 tows of 6 barges each, and 5 canal-boats were either sunk or badly damaged. The following is a list of the vessels reported damaged:

Bark Stadacona,
Bark Anna,
Schooner Mary McCabe,
Schooner Lester A. Lewis,
Schooner Favorite,
Schooner Little Charlie,
Schooner Job H. Jackson,
Schooner S. S. Scranton,
Ferry-boat Maid of Perth,
Tug-boat S. E. Babcock,
Tug-boat Gracie,
Tug-boat Trojan and tow,
Pilot-boat Hope,
Pilot-boat Caldwell H. Colt,
Pilot-boat Thomas D. Harrison,
Pilot-boat Edmund Driggs,
Pilot-boat Ezra Nye,
Lighter International,
Lighter Cement Rock,
Barge Charles N. White,
Two tows of 6 barges each,
Canal-boat Green Mountain,
Canal-boats Nos. 14, 15, 40, and 3065.

NEW JERSEY.

Along the New Jersey coast and in the Horse-shoe at Sandy Hook, 3 schooners, 4 sloops, 5 pilot-boats, 1 barge, and two vessels (names unknown) were damaged:

Schooner Mary Heitman,
Schooner A. B. Crosby,
Sloop Alert,
Sloop Neptune,
Barge Hazeltine,
Two unknown vessels.

At Horse-shoe, Sandy Hook.

Schooner Mayflower,
Sloop P. T. Barnum,
Sloop Pocahontas,
Pilot-boat Edmund Blunt,
Pilot-boat E. H. Williams,
Pilot-boat Centennial,
Pilot-boat W. W. Story,
Pilot-boat Edward Cooper.

DELAWARE RIVER.

In the Delaware River the shipping suffered severely. Of the large fleet of vessels which sought refuge at the Breakwater, scarcely one escaped without damage. Most of those blown ashore at the Breakwater were badly wrecked. From reports received, 1 ship, 3 barks, 2 barkentines, 26 schooners, 2 pilot-boats, and 3 tugs were damaged:

Ship Esther Roy,
Bark Bremiga,
Bark Giacomo Mortola,
Bark Vanadis,
Schooner E. G. Irwin,
Schooner W. H. Rutan,
Schooner Rebecca F. Lamdin,
Schooner Benjamin C. Cromwell,
Schooner Irene Crawford,
Schooner Kocheco,
Schooner Howard Williams,
Schooner William C. Wickham,
Schooner Windsor,

At the Breakwater.

Barkentine Zephyr,
Barkentine Eva Lynch,
Schooner Allie H. Belden,
Schooner Elliot L. Dow,
Schooner John Proctor,
Schooner Hester A. Seward,
Schooner Rebecca M. Smith,
Schooner Abbie P. Cranmer,
Schooner Paul & Thompson,
Schooner George L. Fessenden,
Schooner Isabel Alberto,
Schooner Earl P. Mason,
Schooner Flora A. Newcomb,
Schooner Elizabeth S. Lee,
Schooner George W. Anderson,
Schooner Providence,
Schooner Lizzie V. Hall,
Schooner Index,
Schooner William G. Bartlett,
Pilot-boat C. W. Tunnell,
Pilot-boat Enoch Turley,
Tug-boat George J. Simpson,
Tug-boat Lizzie Crawford,
Tug-boat Tempest.

MARYLAND AND VIRGINIA.

In the harbor of Baltimore there was no material loss. In consequence of the strong NW. gale the water in the harbor was lower than it has ever been in the memory of the oldest steam-boat men. Ferry-boat travel was interrupted; steamers at the Pratt and Light street wharves at the head of the harbor were lying in the mud; ocean steamers at the lower-harbor wharves stopped loading; but on Wednesday, the 14th, the *Oregon*, drawing 24 feet 9 inches, left the harbor without difficulty.

The inclosed list gives the names, so far as can be found, of only the vessels actually reported as having been damaged in the Chesapeake Bay and its tributaries, and is by no means a complete record of the loss to the small dredgers and fishing-boats in the bay. Both sides of the bay seem to have suffered alike, and even in the harbors on the eastern shore, considered very safe ones, the loss was great.

The number of lives lost in the bay and its tributaries was not less than twenty, all incident to the loss of shipping.

The following list gives the names of 2 barks, 78 schooners, and 17 sloops sunk, wrecked, or badly damaged:

Sunk or totally wrecked.

Schooner Harriet Ann,
Schooner C. O. Dougherty,
Schooner West Wind,
Schooner W. P. Hines,
Schooner Mohawk,
Schooner Fire-fly,
Schooner Little John,
Schooner Long Line,
Schooner Eastern Light,
Schooner Canton,
Schooner Antietam,
Schooner Leading Breeze,
Schooner William Turner,
Schooner Wenonah,
Schooner Galena,
Schooner M. J. Marden,
Schooner Constitution,
Schooner Vineyard,
Schooner Queen,
Schooner Gypsy,
Sloop Fire-fly,
Sloop T. T. Francis,
Sloop Flying Trapeze,
Sloop Lavinia North.

Blown ashore and badly damaged.

Bark Henry Warner,
Bark Harvester,
Schooner Fanny Southard,
Schooner Brunette,
Schooner Wm. T. Goldsborough,
Schooner Solomon F. Kerwin,
Schooner Daniel Brown,
Schooner Georgia,
Schooner Annie Jones,
Schooner Caroline,
Schooner Cornelia,
Schooner Frolic.
Schooner Hugh Bolton,
Schooner Three Sisters,
Schooner Edward Cobb,
Schooner William Schmuck,
Schooner Stephen Chase,
Schooner Frank Bateman,
Schooner Thomas Hooper,
Schooner Kate Lawson,
Schooner Mary E. Dennis,
Schooner Alonzo Lee,
Schooner Shearwater,
Schooner American Yacht,
Schooner Lancelot,
Schooner Carrie M. Mass,
Schooner Ann R. Rodgers,
Schooner Cape Charles,
Schooner Commodore,
Schooner Cromwell,
Schooner Eva,
Schooner S. T. Muir,
Schooner Ella Davis,
Schooner Buffalo,
Schooner Maud S.,
Schooner Anna Brown,
Schooner George Lewmon,
Schooner Mary Virginia,
Schooner Cleveland,
Schooner Augusta,
Schooner Bratten,
Schooner Ocean Bird.
Schooner William B. Price,
Schooner A. H. Schultz,
Schooner C. A. Brown,
Schooner Mary E. Coulborn,
Schooner Mary C. Ward,
Schooner Sea View,
Schooner John J. Bell,
Schooner Lydia Sanderson,
Schooner Greyhound,
Schooner Fashion,
Schooner Eva Alice,
Schooner Mount Vernon,
Schooner Emma,
Schooner Hattie Estelle,
Schooner Lizzie and Mirrie,
Schooner Nena May.
Schooner Qui Vive,
Sloop Humming Bird.
Sloop Lizzie,
Sloop Lady Mollie E. Leonard.
Sloop Little Dorrit,
Sloop Daniel H. Mayne,
Sloop Fleetwing.
Sloop O. C. Summers,
Sloop Thomas R. Powley,
Sloop Anna Peterson,
Sloop Howard T. Leach,
Sloop Fly,
Sloop Lydia,
Sloop Lucy V. Fletcher.

SOUTH OF HATTERAS.

Very little damage was done to shipping in the sounds and along the coast of North Carolina, or farther south, the only report received being that of the schooner Aid, sunk at the wharf at Columbus, Ga.

LOST AT SEA WEST OF 40° WEST LONGITUDE.

Bark Johanna,
Bark Cortesia,
Bark Nausika,
Schooner W. L. White,
Schooner Alice Montgomery,
Schooner James Ford.

VESSELS MISSING AND PROBABLY LOST.

Schooner John F. Merrow,
Schooner Henry S. Culver,
Schooner William G. Lewis,
Schooner Rachel Ann Collins,
Fishing-smack Peter Cooper,
Yacht Cythera,
Pilot-boat Phantom,
Pilot-boat Enchantress.

DETAILED STORM REPORTS.

With the exception of a few reports quoted in full in the text, the following list is complete. It is arranged alphabetically by names of vessels, and contains all detailed storm reports at hand from vessels within the area charted at any time during the four days under consideration, with the exception stated above. Barometer readings have been corrected by means of a recent comparison with standard, unless otherwise noted.

American bark Adam W. Spies, Captain Field.

March 14.—Position at noon, latitude 25° 11' N., longitude 64° 22' W. Wind W. by S., 8, veering to WNW. on the 15th, and continuing from same direction till noon of the 16th.

March 16.—Position at noon, latitude 25° 43' N., longitude 65° 17' W.

This was the same westerly gale experienced by the *Wakefield*.

British steam-ship Ailsa, Captain Evans.

March 11.—Gale set in from S., shifting to W., NW., and NE.

March 14.—7 a. m.: Latitude 37° 7' N., longitude 71° W., barometer 29.891.

March 15.—Gale ended; highest force of wind, 10.

British steam-ship Andes, Captain Klinkshel.

(Southward-bound, along the meridian of about 73° 40' W. Position at 11 p. m., March 11, about 100 miles NE by E. from Hatteras.)

Date.	Hour.	Wind.	Barometer.	Temperature.		Remarks.
				Air.	Water.	
Mar. 11	4 a. m.	SE. 4-6	[illegible]			
	Noon		[illegible]			Latitude 37° 19' N., longitude 73° 45' W. Wind very moderate.
	4 p. m.	SSE.	[illegible]	54	54	Wind increasing and squally.
	8 p. m.		29.57			Wind blowing a gale and increasing.
	9 p. m.		[illegible]	54	54	Lowest barometer.
	10 p. m.	SSE.				Strong gale, increasing, and heavy sea from SE.
	11 p. m.					Wind died out, and for 15 minutes there was a dead calm, with the sky very dark and threatening; very heavy squalls of rain; barometer steady at 29.35 (lowest); the wind then jumped out from WNW. and blew with hurricane force; barometer commenced to rise.
Mar. 12	Midnight		29.62			Rising rapidly.
	4 a. m.	NW.	[illegible]	58	60	Hard gale, with a tremendous heavy sea and fierce squalls. Gale continuing with unabated force.
	6 a. m.		[illegible]			
	Noon					Latitude 34° 20' N., longitude 73° 42' W. Very heavy gale and sea; sky covered; barometer rising.
	6 p. m.	NW.	[illegible]			Weather still unsettled, the wind continued to decrease in force and the barometer to rise until midnight, when it registered 29.98. It then commenced to fall slightly and wind to increase to moderate gale, and continued squally and unsettled throughout March 13.
Mar. 13	Noon					Latitude 30° 23' N., longitude 73° 36' W. High westerly winds and squally weather continued until 12 p. m., March 14; then fine weather throughout rest of passage.

American schooner **Anita, Captain Small.**

March 13.—8 a. m.: Gale from NNW.
March 14.—4 a. m.: Latitude 33° N., longitude 78° 24' W. Barometer 29.83 (lowest).
March 16.—8 p. m.: Storm ended. Highest force of wind, 10; shifts of wind, NNW., NW., SW.

German ship **Anna, Captain Menkens.**

March 11.—7 a. m.: Latitude 39° 47' N., longitude 58° 16' W.; wind ENE., 9; barometer 29.90; squally and rainy.
March 12.—7 a. m.: Latitude 40° 3' N., longitude 56° 20' W.; wind ENE., 7 to 8; barometer 30.12; overcast and squally.
March 13.—7 a. m.: Latitude 40° 48' N., longitude 55° 37' W.; wind ESE., 8; barometer 29.77; overcast and gloomy.
March 14.—3 a. m.: Latitude 41° 10' N., longitude 54° 30' W.; barometer 29° 57' (lowest). 7 a. m.: Latitude 41° 16' N., longitude 54° 38' W.; wind, W. by N., 4; barometer 29.67; rainy. Noon: Calm; then light southerly winds, 6 hours of rain, thunder and lightning. 3 p. m.: Heavy squalls, with heavy rain.
March 15.—Calms and light southerly and westerly winds, with heavy squalls and a great deal of rain, lightning, and thunder. 7 a. m.: Latitude 41° 23' N., longitude 53° 42' W.; wind SSE., 3; barometer 29.64; gloomy.
March 16.—Gale set in from the NW., and for ten hours blew a whole gale, with very heavy squalls and rain; very high sea. 7 a. m.: Latitude 41° 43' N., longitude 53° 47' W.; wind SW., 2; barometer 29.04; clearing. 11 a. m.: Latitude 41° 46' N., longitude 53° 30' W.; barometer 28.91 (lowest).

American ship **Annie M. Small, Captain Bailey.**

(Voyage from Colombo, Ceylon, to New York.)

March 11.—Midnight to 4 a. m.: Fresh breeze and dull overcast sky. 5 a. m.: Went out of the stream, hauled up NNE., and went in again. 6 a. m.: Barometer 30.11; chopping cross-sea all night; wind SE., 5. 10 a. m.: Fresh and quite fine for a SE. wind; went out of the stream again on a N. by E. course, and the sea got smooth at once; barometer 30.06. Noon: Latitude 36° 38' N., longitude 74° 9' W.; barometer 30.02. 2 p. m.: Wind SE., 5; barometer 29.98. 4 p. m.: Barometer 29.86. 6 p. m.: Barometer 29.76, wind increasing to force 6. 10 p. m.: Wind still at SE., force 7; barometer 29.71; sails furled to lower topsails, foresail, and upper main-topsail; weather thick and rainy. Midnight: Barometer 29.64; course all day between N. and NNE.
March 12.—2 a. m.: Wind shifted to NNW., force 11 to 12; barometer 29.61, but at 4 a. m. fell to 29.35, then steadily rising until noon, when, in latitude 39° N., longitude 73° 40' W., it reached 29.51; barometer record ended here. At 2 a. m., when wind shifted to NNW., braced around, clewed down upper main-topsail and hauled up foresail and mizzen-topsail and sent men to furl them, but gale increased to a hurricane and blew them to pieces, also blowing lower foretopsail away, and main-topsail yard broke short off in the slings. We also lost both topsails. Terrific gale and blinding snow, ship lying on beam-ends with yard-arms in water and making water fast. Ship covered with snow, and ice making fast. At 10 a. m. shipped a sea which took two boats, one man, and everything about decks; saved the man; five men with hands and feet frost-bitten and three injured by washing about; all hands lashed to pumps and working them continually. All rooms and galley washed out; ship lying with hatch-coamings under water. Cargo shifted at 8 p. m.; wheel-shaft broke, and steering-gear completely smashed; secured rudder with tackle as well as possible. Foreyard sprung, main yard gone at sheave-hole, and the remainder of sails cut from the yards to keep ship to wind. Tarpaulin in mizzen rigging. Midnight: Gale still raging and frightful sea; oil-bags over, which work well for the NW. sea, but have no effect on the NE. and SE. sea. Pumps still going, but don't gain any; 4 feet of water in the ship; snowing hard all the time. This is the worst gale I ever experienced; ship making bad work of it and straining badly. Eight men unfit for duty; bad outlook; covered with snow and ice. Hard luck!
March 13.—Midnight to 8 a. m.: No change, still snowing, and gale as bad as ever; ship straining badly, and can't gain any on the pumps, working them continually as well as we can with a disabled crew; sea very bad, making a clean breach over the ship; at daylight a little less wind, and sea more regular; still snowing. Noon: Moderating. At 3 p. m.: Set upper foretopsail and jib; managed to get before the wind; lost the jib. I intend to run for warm water and thaw out; steering with tackles on tiller; pumps going constantly, no suck; ship has about 4 feet list to starboard and steers badly. Bent spare lower foretopsail and set it. More moderate at midnight. No suck on the pumps, but the water don't gain any on us; all right. Heavy snow squalls. Large sea from N. My hands are swelled so I can hardly hold a pen.

British steam-ship **Baltimore, Captain Trenery.**

Date.	Lat. N.	Long. W.	Barometer. Noon.	Barometer. Mid-night.	Temperature. Air.	Temperature. Water.	Wind. A. M.		Wind. P. M.		Sea.	Remarks.
Mar. 11	41 20	60 52		29.97		50	NE.	8	NE.	7	H.	
12	41 56	64 36	29.62	29.72	34	46	ENE.	8	SE.	6	M.	Rainy.
13	41 26	66 55	29.47	29.82	40	45	W.	5	Var.	5	M.	Snow.
14	39 41	70 23	29.83	29.82	40	36	Var.	5	NNE.	5	M.	Snow.

British steam-ship Benison, Captain Aitkenhead.

March 13.—Position at noon, latitude 37° 57′ N., longitude 63° 02′ W. Gale set in from NW., 8, shifting at noon to W.; barometer 29.48.

March 14.—Position at noon, latitude 39° 06′ N., longitude 65° 10′ W. Wind backed to NW. by N., continuing till 5 p. m., when it was NNE., 8 to 7; barometer at noon, 29.41.

March 15.—Position at noon, latitude 39° 46′ N., longitude 67° 17′ W. Continuation of gale from NE. to NE. by E., 9 to 10, and moderating; barometer 29.62.

British steam-ship Brooklyn City, Captain Fitt.

March 11.—11.30 p. m.: Latitude 40° 35′ N., longitude 67° 27′ W.; wind ESE., 8; barometer 30.

March 12.—3.30 a. m.: Wind ESE., 8; barometer 29.85; heavy sea. 7.30 a. m.: Wind ESE., 9; barometer 29.80. 11.30 a. m.: Latitude 40° 45′ N., longitude 65° 39′ W.; squally, with heavy rain; wind ESE., 9; barometer 29.70. 4 p. m.: Wind ESE., 10; barometer 29.55; heavy sea, rainy. 7.30 p. m.: Latitude 40° 45′ N., longitude 64° 40′ W.; wind SE., 10; barometer 29.40. 11 p. m.: Wind veered to W.; high, confused sea. [The barometer continued to fall after shift of wind, but the wind from W. seems to be noticeably less severe than from SE. (before shift), probably in large part due to the fact that the vessel was steaming to the eastward.] 11.30 p. m.: Latitude 40° 53′ N., longitude 64° 20′ W.; wind W., 7; barometer 29.35.

March 13.—3.30 a. m.: Wind W., 6; barometer 29.36; overcast; high confused sea. 7.30 a. m.: Wind W., 5; barometer 29.38. 11.30 a. m.: Latitude 40° 53′ N., longitude 62° 51′ W.; wind W., 5; barometer 29.40 and rising.

British steam-ship Caribbean, Captain Daniel.

March 12.—Gale set in from SSE., 8. Noon position, latitude 35° N., longitude 63° W. Barometer 29.30, lowest. Moderated at midnight.

German steam-ship Catania, Captain Franck.

(Baltimore to Rio Janeiro.)

March 11.—About 200 miles SW. by W. from Bermuda. At 7.30 a. m., light breeze from ESE.; fine weather; barometer 30.22. Wind then died away.

March 12.—From morning to afternoon, strong gale from SSW., shifting to W. and NW. Heavy rain during night, followed by fine weather and moderate sea. Lowest barometer at 3 p. m., 29.71, in latitude 28° 30′ N., longitude 65° 50′ W. Gale lasted only a few hours. Highest force of wind, 10.

March 13.—Light, variable winds, fine weather, and high rolling sea from NNW.

New York pilot-boat Charles H. Marshall (No. 3).

(Report communicated by Boat-keeper Robinson, in behalf of the pilots of No. 3.)

March 10.—A. M.: Left Staten Island on a cruise to the southward; moderate breeze from ENE., which continued all day. At 7 p. m. we hove to, with the Highland Light in sight, bearing NNW. distant 18 miles. At 8 p. m. the wind began to increase and it commenced to rain; double-reefed the sails and lay hove-to all night.

March 11.—At 4 a. m. the wind had moderated considerably, and, as it hauled more to the southward, put all sail on the boat and steered to the south in company with No. 4 and No. 6. At 7.30 a. m. put Pilot Ackerman on board of an inward-bound vessel. At 9 a. m. it commenced to blow from SE., so concluded to go no farther to the southward. Put single reefs in all sails and laid to for about an hour; were then about 18 miles E. by S. from Barnegat Light. At 10 a. m. the pilots, who are good judges of the weather, thought by the threatening weather that there was going to be a storm, but not so bad a one as it proved to be. Put two more reefs in the sails and steered to the northward, intending to go in for harbor if possible. At 4 p. m. it was blowing a moderate gale from SE., increasing at 5 p. m. to a strong gale, when put three reefs in the mainsail and furled the jib; were then about 12 miles SE. from the light-ship; but it shut down a dense fog, so would not run in, but concluded to stop out and take it as it came, which it did. Hove to on the starboard tack, heading to the eastward, remaining that way until 2 a. m., March 12.

March 12.—At 2 a. m. wore around, the wind hauling to the east. At 3 a. m. the wind moderated, but the weather looked so threatening in the NW. that the fourth reef was taken in the mainsail and treble reefed the foresail. At 3.30 a. m. the wind died out completely, and the boat lay broadside on to the heavy SE. sea, which was threatening every minute to engulf the little craft; but she did not have to wait long for wind, for at 3.55 a. m., at which time were about 12 miles ESE. from Sandy Hook Light-ship, it came out from the NW. with such force that the boat went over on her beam ends, but righted again immediately. In two hours the boat was so much iced up by the snow and water that struck her that she resembled a small iceberg. At 8 a. m. the wind increased to a hurricane. Had to lower the foresail, but before the sail could be hauled down had to get iron bars and sledge-hammers to beat the ice off the ropes and mast, and even then only got it down about half-way, so had to lash it up with ropes the best way possible, to save it from blowing away. Then hauled down the fore stay-sail and did the same thing with it, much at the risk of the lives of the crew, for the seas by this time were running in every direction, owing to the NW. sea coming down in contact with the one from SE. The little vessel was in danger of being swamped, for no one but those who were out in that blizzard and saw those large breaking seas coming down on top of her know what danger she was in. At 10 a. m. the snow and rain came with such force that it was impossible to look to windward, and the boat was lying broadside on to the sea, heading about SW.* At 10.30 a. m. Captain Partridge proposed that a drag of some kind should be put out to help keep the boat head to sea. So took the hawser, which was of 5-inch rope and [illegible] fathoms in length, and put a sling upon the anchor pole (which was a heavy piece of teakwood 16 feet long, 5 inches in diameter, and iron bound), then took the hawser through the hawse-pipe and bent it to the sling on the pole; then lashing the two windlass brakes and a small kedge anchor to the pole, hove it overboard, paying out the full length of the hawser. This checked the boat a little, but did not have the desired effect. It was certain that something must be done to save the boat, so oil was proposed, and three oil-bags were made out of duck, about 20 by 14 inches, and half filled with oakum saturated with oil. These were put over the side, one forward, one amidships, and one on the weather quarter. This is positively what saved the boat and the crew's lives, for the oil would break the sea and nothing but the swell would remain, which was bad enough itself. The boat still continued to lie broadside on to the sea, and another drag was proposed, consisting of the working anchor and [illegible] fathoms of 4 inch rope; the stock of the anchor was lashed to the shank to prevent its holding on the bottom; then, putting a long sling on it, it was let go, but not without a perilous struggle. This kept her head up a little more to the sea, and gave a little more assurance of safety. One of the oil-bags washed inboard, so a heavy iron bolt was put in it to keep it in the water; this being a success, the same was done to the other two bags. While lying there fighting for life against the gale the oil bags were filled every half hour with fresh oil, and it was expected every moment that some passing vessel would run the boat down, for one could not see from one end of her to the other; but trusting in Providence to pull her safely through, not one man on board showed the least sign of fear, the feelings of each one known only to himself. When it got dark on the evening of the 12th† the boat looked like a wreck, being encased in ice; it was not expected that she would live until daylight, but continued replenishing the oil-bags every half hour during the night, the members of the crew taking turn and turn about to go on deck to haul them in, taking care, however, that each man had a rope around him as a precaution against being washed overboard, for it was necessary to crawl on hands and knees along the deck to reach the bags. No one on board slept that night. At 11.45 p. m. a heavy sea struck the boat and sent her over on her side, shifting everything that was movable down below, sending all flying to leeward; the water rushed down the forward hatch, and it was thought all were lost, when all of a sudden the little boat righted again; but had another sea struck her at that time she would have been done for.

March 13.—Blowing the same, with squalls that came down shrieking as though they would lift the boat out of water. Going forward at 5 a. m. to inspect the oil-bags, discovered that both the hawsers were gone at the hawse-holes, but did not make this known to the crew at once for fear of making them uneasy. At noon, however, it brightened up to the westward, and at 4 p. m. it moderated; but the foresail could not be set, it was frozen so hard, but the storm try-sail was bent and set instead, and the boat came up more head to the sea. At 5 p. m. drifted on top of a pilot boat's broken mast (No. [illegible]), and there was a very discouraging sight; but it was shoved clear with a boat hook. At 6 p. m. wore around to the northward, but not before considering the risk that would be run of the boat foundering on account of the great weight of ice; but she got around, her deck being swept, however, upon broaching to, and one man was nearly washed overboard, but escaped with a bruised arm. At 7 p. m. commenced to start to clear the ice off the fore stay-sail. After three and a half hours' hard work the sail was set and the boat rendered safe.

March 14.—Clear and moderate weather. After five hours' work the sails and spars were cleared of ice, and with all sail set and a moderate breeze stood to the westward. Steered NNW. for 30 miles, and made Jersey Beach [illegible] miles to the southward of the Highlands, after drifting over 150 miles in forty-eight hours. By nightfall, although all were worn out by fatigue, resumed station on the bar, arriving there at 4 a. m. on the 15th.

March 15.—At 5.30 a. m. spoke pilot boat No. 16, and learned that several pilot-boats had been lost and several more were still at sea, the Maxwell being the first one that had arrived. The faces and hands of all the crew were badly frost bitten; all the oil, coal, wood, and many other supplies had given out; for no matter how much coal was put on the fire but little heat was felt, not enough to dry the clothes, so all on board had to keep on their wet clothes throughout the storm, which was far from comfortable. The boat sustained no damage beyond the loss of the anchor and hawsers, and all were glad to escape so easily. The barometer gave no sign of the approaching blizzard until about fifteen minutes after it had struck, when it fell .1 for a few minutes, when it went up again to its old place, .1 above "change" (29.50). The lowest barometer was about [illegible].

* Ran SSW. 15 miles from 4 to 10.30 a. m. on the 12th.

† At 4 p. m. was [illegible] miles ESE. from Sandy Hook Lightship.

British steam-ship City of Chester, Captain Lewis.

Date.	Hour.	Wind.		Barometer.	Temperature.		Remarks.
					Air.	Water.	
Mar. 11.	Noon ...	E.	6	......	......	......	Latitude 40° 23' N., longitude 70° 20' W.
	2 p. m. ...	E.	6	29.98	38	37	
	4 p. m. ...	E.	6	29.95	38	37	
	6 p. m. ...	E.	6	29.86	39	39	
	8 p. m. ...	E.	6	29.78	46	44	
	10 p. m. ..	E.	6	29.72	48	45	
	Midnight	E.	6	29.70	48	45	Strong head-sea throughout.
Mar. 12.	2 a. m. ...	E.	6	29.73	48	42	
	4 a. m. ...	E.	6	29.46	41	49	
	6 a. m. ...	ESE.	7	29.48	47	45	
	8 a. m. ...	ESE.	7	29.41	50	50	
	10 a. m. ..	ESE.	7	29.43	53	58	
	Noon ...	ESE.	7	29.48	62	58	Latitude 40° 23' N., longitude 66° 8' W.
	2 p. m. ...	ESE.	7	29.49	62	60	
	6 p. m. ...	ESE.	7	29.55	51	58	
	8 p. m. ...	ESE.	7	29.50	54	60	
	12 p. m. ...	ESE.	7	29.53	62	60	Rough head-sea throughout.
Mar. 13.	2 a. m. ...	ESE.	9	29.48	52	58	
	4 a. m. ..	ESE.	6	29.28	54	62	
	8 a. m. ...	ESE.	7	29.31	55	62	
	10 a. m. ...	ESE.	7	29.22	55	[illegible]	
	Noon ...	ESE.	7	29.24	55	66	Latitude 40° 21' N., longitude 66° 38' W. (?)
	2 p. m. ...	ESE.	7	29.27	55	59	Very heavy head-sea.
	4 p. m. ...	ESE.	7	29.30	56	67	
	6 p. m. ...	ESE.	7	29.35	58	63	
	8 p. m. ...	ESE.	7	29.41	58	63	
	10 p. m. ...	ESE.	6	29.43	58	61	
	Midnight	ESE.	6	29.45	59	63	

British steam-ship City of Lincoln, Captain Fry.

March 14.—Gale set in from WSW., shifting to WNW., highest force 10. 8.48 p. m.: Latitude 31° 44' N., longitude 63° 38' W.; barometer 29.51, lowest.

March 16.—Moderated.

American steam-ship Colon, Captain Henderson.

March 11.—Experienced a severe gale, commencing at SE. and shifting suddenly to the westward and NW. Very heavy, confused sea, heaviest from the northward. Violent squalls from the NNW., with much rain and hail, and thick weather; ending with clear weather at NNW. At 11.03 p. m., in latitude 35° 20' N., longitude 74° W., barometer 29.60, lowest.

March 12.—Gale moderated.

German ship *Dora*, Captain Meyer.

The report from this vessel was received too late to be used in the preparation of this monograph, but the following abstract will be found of interest:

Date.	Hour.	Wind.		Barometer.	Remarks.
Mar. 10	Midnight	NNW.	9	30.19	Squally, rainy; high sea from NNW.
Mar. 11	Forenoon	NNW.	9-7	......	Wind, weather, and sea showing tendency to moderate.
	Noon	NNW.	7	30.1[illegible]	Latitude 39° [illegible]' N., longitude 61° 17' W. Weather same.
Mar. 12	Forenoon	NNW.		......	Barometer falling rapidly; wind moderate and hauling to westward.
	Noon	SW.	7	29.7[illegible]	Overcast, and passing showers; wind increasing. Latitude 39° 1[illegible]' N., longitude 6[illegible]° 2[illegible]' W.
	8 p. m.	SSW.	10	29.36	
	Midnight	SSW.	11	29.3[illegible]	Steady rain; very high sea from SW.
Mar. 13	4 a. m.	NW.	6	29.4[illegible]	Weather same; sea moderating.
	6 a. m.	WNW.		......	Moderating; wind veering to W. and NW.; barometer rising.
	Noon			29.5[illegible]	Latitude 38° 56' N., longitude [illegible]° 49' W. Barometer steady until midnight.
Mar. 14	Noon	SW.	3	29.6[illegible]	Barometer falling slowly; light swell from westward; overcast and cloudy. Latitude 39° 56' N., longitude 60° 3[illegible]' W.

Pilot-boat Edward E. Barrett.

(Report communicated by Pilot Charles E. Hughes.)

March 10.—Noon: Latitude 40° 30' N., longitude 6[illegible]° 10' W.; wind NNE.; fresh breeze and very clear; barometer 30.61. 8 p. m.: Latitude 40° 50' N., longitude 67° W.; wind NE. by N.; moderate breeze all night; clear. Midnight: Wind light from ENE. to E.; barometer 30.41.

March 11.—4 a. m. Wind ENE.; clear, mild weather; barometer 30.36. 8 a. m.: Wind E., freshening up toward noon. Noon: Latitude 40° 52' N., longitude 67° 40' W.; barometer 30.36. 8 p. m.: Latitude 40° 50' N., longitude 67° 55' W.; slightly cloudy overhead, with very clear horizon; barometer 30.21; wind from E. to E. by N., toward midnight hauling E.

March 12.—4 a. m.: Wind from E. to E. by S.; cloudy, and breeze freshening; boat running W.; barometer 29.86. 7 a. m.: Wind E. by S.; barometer 29.71, and falling steadily; boat running under double-reefed foresail and head of fore stay-sail. 8 a. m.: Wind ESE.; commenced raining; barometer 29.61; bent main try-sail and frapped jib; running W. ½ S.; continued thick and rainy, with a heavy sea getting up from the eastward. 11.30 a. m.: Blowing heavy, with very heavy gusts of wind, and rain squalls; barometer 29.31; set main try-sail, laffed to, furled foresail, bent fore try-sail and set it, furling main try-sail; squared away W. by N. Noon: Latitude 40° 30' N., longitude 70° W., both by dead reckoning; barometer 29.26. 1 p. m.: Wind moderating; set fore stay-sail and main try-sail; heavy cross-sea from S. to SW. and W.; wind hauling SE. and then, baffling, to SSE., dying out; rain squalls; barometer 29.11; boat headed to westward. 7 p. m.: Wind hauled to NW.; moderate breeze, with light drizzling rain. 7.30 p. m.: Blowing heavy from W., with snow; furled main try-sail and fore stay-sail; wore ship head to southward, heading from S. to SSW., lying under fore try-sail; continued to blow very heavy, with heavy squalls, until midnight; wind from W. to W. by S. and WSW., with thick snow-storm, and freezing hard; heavy cross-sea from WSW. and E. Midnight: Sea coming from W. to SW., easterly sea having run down; latitude 40° 30' N., longitude 70° 35' W.; barometer 29.21.

March 13.—4 a. m.: Wind WSW., with snow-squalls, and freezing; heavy sea from SW. to W.; barometer 29.21, oscillating from 29.16 to 29.26. 7 a. m.: Wind SW. to SW. by W., moderating; wore ship to the northward; barometer 29.31. 8 a. m.: Set head of fore stay-sail; boat head-reaching and heading up from NW. by W. to NW. by N. Noon: Latitude 40° 21' N., longitude 70° 15' W.; wind SW., moderating, with occasional snow-squalls; sea going down fast; barometer 29.41. 4 p. m.: Moderating to a light breeze, hauling around to NE. by way of S. and then to N.; through night dying out to a calm; snow.

American schooner Ellen M. Golder, Captain Johnson.

March 11.—6 p. m.: Barnegat, WSW. 18 miles; wind SE., 6. Noon: Wind ESE., 7. 6 p. m.: Wind ESE., 8; barometer 29.44; weather perfectly dry, sky slightly overcast. 8 p. m.: Half-way between Shinnecock and Fire Island, 14 miles off shore; wind backing to NE., 8.

March 12.—4 a. m.: 18 miles off shore and standing to the SE., hove to. 5 a. m.: Wind NE., 9; soon commenced to blow heavy from NNE. to N. 10, snowing hard; barometer 29.12 and falling. 10 a. m.: Wind NW., 12. 2 p. m.: Barometer vibrating between 29.09 and 29.07.

March 13.—Noon: Position by dead reckoning, latitude 39° 58' N., longitude 73° 30' W. The gale moderated just after midnight, when the barometer was about 29.19.

British brig Energy, Captain McBride.

March 12.—Latitude 25° 38′ N., longitude 68° 50′ W.; wind S. to SSW., 7, veering about 2 p. m. to NW., 8, continuing throughout the day from NW. to NNE., and back to NW. by W.; barometer at noon 29.86.

March 13.—Wind NW. to W., 8 to 10.

March 14.—Wind NW., 10 to 12.

March 15.—Latitude 28° 40′ N., longitude 68° 5′ W.; moderated.

British steam-ship Erl King, Captain Priske.

March 11.—Position at noon, latitude 34° 48′ N., longitude 47° 52′ W.; moderate breeze and light squalls, with sharp showers of rain; wind veering from SW. to W. During afternoon wind increased to a fresh gale from SW., with heavy squalls, rain, and very heavy sea; vessel pitching, water keeping decks continually flooded. At midnight a heavy gale, continuing with succession of squalls, blowing with hurricane force; heavy rain.

March 12.—Noon position, latitude 32° 28′ N., longitude 51° 18′ W.; heavy gale, continuing with violent squalls of rain and terrific head-sea, decreasing during afternoon to a strong breeze with clear weather and heavy sea.

NOTE.—The hurricane encountered by this vessel was that shown to the eastward of Bermuda on the Weather Charts of the 11th and 12th. No report of the weather experienced during the 13th and 14th, when she must have felt the effects of the great storm, has been received as yet.

Norwegian steam ship Faedrelandet, Captain Brunn.

March 12.—Gale set in from SSW. and shifted suddenly by way of W. to NNW. in a heavy rain shower. Position at 7 a. m., latitude 28° N., longitude 74° 3′ west.

March 12.—At 5 a. m., in latitude 30° 20′ N., longitude 75° W.; barometer, 29.80.

March 13.—Wind NW. by N., 10.

March 14.—4 a. m.: In latitude 33° 30′ N., longitude 75° 5′ W.; barometer 29.72. Between 4 and 8 a. m. the air had a very ugly appearance, stormy looking, and had a numerous lot of small waterspouts and masses of dripping fog coming from the water; temperature of water was about 72 and the air 46.

British steam-ship Furnessia, Capt. J. Hedderwick.

March 12.—Gale set in from N.; shifted from N. by W. to NNW. and NW.

March 13.—7.45 a. m.: Latitude 39° 24′ N., longitude 71° 47′ W.; barometer 29.26. 8.30 a. m.: gale abated; highest force 11.

British ship Glenburn, Captain Johansen.

(At New York, March 30, from Calcutta.)

[NOTE.—The log being kept by sea time, it follows that afternoon observations are for the preceding civil date; for forenoon observations civil date is the same as that given in the log.]

March 8.—P. M.: Moderate W. and NW. wind and light showers of rain; barometer 29.95. 4 p. m.: Moderate W. and NW. wind and light showers of rain; barometer 29.95. 8 p. m.: Calm and light variable air, sky overcast and gloomy; barometer 29.99. Midnight: Light to SE. to SW. winds, sky overcast and gloomy; barometer 29.99. 4 a. m.: Fresh SW. winds and gloomy; barometer 29.95. 8 a. m.: Fresh SW. winds and heavy rain; barometer 29.92. Noon: Latitude 31° 19′ N., longitude 58° 29′ W.; fresh WSW. winds and dull, with a heavy NW. swell.

March 9.—P. M.: Fresh WSW. winds and dull; barometer 29.85. 4 p. m.: Fresh WSW. winds and dull; barometer 29.85. 8 p. m.: Light NW. winds and cloudy; barometer 29.86. Midnight: Moderate NW. winds and clear; barometer 29.95. 4 a. m.: Squally; barometer 29.88. 8 a. m.: Fresh winds and squally; barometer 29.96. Noon: Latitude 31° 8′ N., longitude 59° 38′ W.; strong NW. wind and squally.

March 10.—P. M.: Strong NW. wind and squally; barometer 29.96. 4 p. m.: NW. winds and fierce squalls; barometer 29.97. 8 p. m.: Strong WNW. winds, with fierce squalls and heavy rain; barometer 30.03. Midnight: Strong WNW. winds, hard squalls, with heavy rain; barometer 30. 4 a. m.: Barometer 29.98. 8 a. m.: Fresh winds and clear; barometer 29.99. Noon: Latitude 31° 54′ N., longitude 59° 18′ W.; strong WNW. winds and squally.

March 11.—P. M.: Strong WNW. wind and squally; barometer 30. 4 p. m.: barometer 29.99. 8 p. m.: Fresh gale, hard squalls, and wind; barometer 29.98. Midnight: Hard gale, with fierce squalls; barometer 29.91. 4 a. m.: barometer 29.93. 8 a. m.: NW. gale and squally; barometer 29.93. Noon: Latitude 32° 49′ N., longitude 58° 58′ W.; hard NW. gale and violent squalls.

March 12.—P. M.: Hard gale and violent squalls; barometer 29.98. 4 p. m.: Fresh NW. gale and clear; barometer 29.95. 8 p. m.: Moderate NW. gale; barometer 30.01. Midnight: Moderate to light wind from NNW. to WNW. and overcast; barometer 30.02. 4 a. m.: Light winds and clear; barometer 30. 8 a. m.: Light winds and clear; barometer 30.02. Noon: Latitude 32° 20′ N., longitude 59° 30′ W.; light southerly winds.

March 13.—P. M.: Light southerly winds and clear; barometer 29.90. 4 p. m.: Fresh winds and cloudy, gloomy weather; barometer 29.79. 8 p. m.: Fresh wind, cloudy, gloomy weather, and gusty; barometer 29.76. 9 p. m.: Vivid lightning all around the horizon, with frequent squalls. 10 p. m.: Wind shifted to the westward, with heavy rain. Midnight: Fresh westerly gale, with hard squalls; barometer 29.63. 4 a. m.: Fresh westerly gale, with hard squalls; barometer [illegible]. 8 a. m.: Fresh westerly gale, with hard squalls; barometer 29.64. Noon: Latitude 33° 36′ N., longitude 60° 56′ W.; moderate westerly winds and clear.

March 14.—P. M.: Moderate westerly winds and clear; barometer 29.69. 4 p. m.: Moderate westerly winds and clear; barometer 29.69. 8 p. m.: W. winds and cloudy; barometer 29.69. 11 p. m.: Threatening appearance and vivid lightning to the NW. Midnight: Dull, gloomy weather, with vivid lightning and fierce squalls; barometer 29.68. 4 a. m.: Moderate WSW. winds and gloomy; barometer 29.60. 8 a. m.: SW. winds; barometer 29.68. Noon: Latitude 34° 55′ N., longitude 61° 40′ W.; SW. winds and clear.

March 15.—P. M.: Moderate SW. winds and clear; barometer 29.65. 4 p. m.: Light winds and gloomy; barometer 29.64. 8 p. m.: Vivid lightning all around the horizon; barometer 29.62. Midnight: Vivid lightning all around the horizon; barometer 29.55. 4 a. m.: Vivid lightning all around the horizon; barometer 29.52. 8 a. m.: Fierce squalls; barometer 29.49. Noon: Latitude 35° 07′ N.; longitude 62° 24′ W.; strong NW. gale and broken clouds.

March 16.—P. M.: Strong NW. gale and broken clouds; barometer 29.47. 4 p. m.: Increasing NNW. gale with fierce squalls; barometer 29.49. 8 p. m.: Hard gale and fierce squalls; barometer 29.49. Midnight: Hard NNW. gale and fierce squalls with heavy showers of hail and rain and heavy SW. sea running; barometer 29.54. 4 a. m.: Hard NNW. gale and fierce squalls, with heavy showers of hail and rain, and heavy SW. sea running; barometer 29.61. 8 a. m.: Hard NNW. gale and fierce squalls, with heavy showers of hail and rain, and heavy SW. sea running; barometer 29.77. Noon: Latitude 35° 34′ N.; longitude 63° 02′ W.; strong NW. winds and squally.

March 17.—P. M.: Strong NW. winds and squally; barometer 29.86. 4 p. m.: Strong NW. winds and squally; barometer 29.86. 8 p. m.: Fresh WNW. winds and cloudy, with lightning to the north-northwestward; barometer 29.89.(?) Midnight: Fresh WNW. winds and dull gloomy weather; barometer [illegible]. 4 a. m.: Fresh WNW. to WSW. winds and overcast; barometer 29.87. 8 a. m.: Fresh SW. winds and puffy with rain; barometer [illegible]. Noon: Latitude 35° 14′ N.; longitude [illegible] W.; strong SW. wind and squally with rain and heavy SW. swell.

March 18.—P. M.: Strong SW. winds and squally with rain; barometer 29.75. 4 p. m.: Strong SW. winds and squally with rain; barometer 29.73. 8 p. m.: Strong SSW. gale and black sky, with vivid chain lightning and tremendous loud thunder, with heavy down-pouring of hail and rain; barometer 29.73. Midnight: Strong SSW. gale and black sky, with vivid chain lightning and tremendous loud thunder, with heavy down-pouring of hail and rain; barometer 29.62. 4 a. m.: Strong SSW. gale and black sky, with vivid chain lightning and tremendous loud thunder, with heavy down-pouring of hail and rain, and fierce squalls; barometer 29.55. 8 a. m.: Strong increasing gale; lightning and thunder still keeping up, and heavy SSW. sea; winds from WNW. to SSW.; barometer 29.48. Noon: Latitude 35° 29′ N.; longitude 64° 50′ W.; whole northerly gale, with fierce squalls and hail and rain.

March 19.—P. M.: Whole northerly gale and fierce squalls; barometer 29.48. 4 p. m.: WNW. gale and fierce squalls and heavy hail and rain showers; barometer 29.60. 8 p. m.: WNW. gale and fierce squalls and heavy hail and rain showers; barometer 29.81. Midnight: Hard gale with heavy squalls and hail and rain; barometer 29.85. 4 a. m.: Fresh gale and squally; barometer 29.93. 8 a. m.: Strong NNW. winds and hard squall, with hail and rain. Noon: Latitude 35° 07′ N., longitude 64° 50′ W. Strong winds and squally.

March 20.—P. M.: Strong NNW. wind and puffy; barometer 30.08. 4 p. m.: Strong NNW. wind and puffy; barometer 30.09. 8 p. m.: Moderate winds and cloudy; barometer 30.16. Midnight: Moderate winds and overcast; barometer 30.19. 4 a. m.: Moderate winds and overcast; barometer 30.18. 8 a. m.: Moderate winds and overcast; barometer 30.21. Noon: Latitude 35° 6′ N., longitude 60° 3′ W. Light NW. airs and calm, cloudy weather.

British steam-ship Glenderon, Captain Peterson.

March 10.—4 p. m.: In latitude 38° 50′ N., longitude 60° 37′ W., fresh gale from NNW., 8. Barometer, lowest reading, 29.70. At 10 p. m. sudden shift to NE., and blew a hurricane; continued with force of 12 until 8 a. m., March 11, with steadily rising barometer, when it commenced to moderate.

March 11.—8 p. m.: Fresh breeze from NE.; barometer 30.23.

American schooner Herald, Captain Heagan.

(Northward bound, through the Straits of Florida.)

March 11.—Off Sagua, Cuba; wind WNW. to N., force 8.

March 12.—Latitude 23° 5′ N., longitude 79° 37′ W.; same gale, varying to N. by E., force 9.

March 13.—Latitude 24° 14′ N., longitude 79° 15′ W.; same gale, N. by E. to N., backing to NNW., and moderating for a few hours, afterwards increased again to gale from WNW., force 9, varying to N. and N. by E.

March 14.—Latitude 26° 28′ N., longitude 78° 11′ W.; wind backed to WNW., force 10.

March 15.—Latitude 28° 21′ N., longitude [illegible] 38′ W.; wind WNW., force [illegible], veered to ENE. at noon, and moderated. (No barometer record.)

German bark Johanna, Captain **Meyer.**

(Northward bound, in the Gulf Stream below Hatteras.)

Date.	Hour.	Wind.		Remarks.
Mar. 11	A. M.	Easterly breeze.		
	Noon	S.	4	Latitude 31° 17′ N., longitude 78° 51′ W. Ship running north; wind gradually increasing.
	4 p. m.	S.	7	Had shortened sail in increasing wind.
	6 p. m.	S.	9	Blowing a strong gale and splitting sails.
	8 p. m.	S.	12	Blowing a hurricane, with steady, heavy rain, almost a deluge; still running ship; she would hardly steer; very difficult to keep her before the wind.
	10.30 p. m.	....		Wind shifted suddenly from S. to NW., sea running very high from all directions. Position about latitude 33° 40′ N., longitude 73° 40′ W. Brought ship to wind, and lay to on port tack.
Mar. 12	6 a. m.	NW.	12	Wore ship and lay to on starboard tack, the sea breaking high from every direction. Impossible to run.
	Noon	....		Latitude 33° 20′ N., longitude 74° W.
Mar. 13	Noon	....		Latitude 33° 47′ N., longitude 73° 42′ W.
Mar. 14	Noon	....		Latitude 33° 34′ N., longitude 74° 30′ W. Wind blowing a strong gale, at times in hurricane force, from N. to NW., until March 15. Men working the pumps continually, but water gaining.
Mar. 15	2 p. m.	....		Abandoned the vessel with 7 feet of water in her hold. Lost sight of her at 7 p. m., when she seemed to have settled somewhat and probably went down before morning.

NOTE.—The captain thinks the lowest reading of his barometer was about 28.25 (corrected). The captain of the German bark *Weser*, who rescued the crew, states that the position where she was abandoned was about latitude 32° 27′ N., longitude 73° 15′ W.

American barkentine John J. Marsh, Captain Whittier.

(Bound south, through Windward Channel.)

March 11.—7 a. m.: Latitude 21° 40′ N., longitude 72° 40′ W.; barometer 30.18; wind ENE., 4; clear weather and no rain.

March 12.—7 a. m.: Latitude 20° N., longitude 74° 1′ W.; barometer 30.10; wind SW., 3; clear.

March 13.—7 a. m.: Latitude 19° 45′ N., longitude 75° 10′ W.; barometer 30.10; wind NW. by N., 3; three hours of heavy rain.

March 14.—7 a. m.: Latitude 19° 32′ N., longitude 77.5 W., barometer 30.11; wind ENE., 3; clear weather and no more rain.

American steam-ship; Knickerbocker, Captain Kemble.

(Northward bound; off Hatteras at about noon, March 12.)

Date.	Hour.	Wind.		Barometer.	Temperature.		Remarks.
					Air.	Water.	
Mar. 10	Midnight	SE. by E.	6	30.14	67	77	Cloudy and squally, with passing showers.
Mar. 11	4 a. m.	SE.	7	29.95	79	76	Ship rolling heavily.
	8 a. m.	SE. by S.	7	29.90	68	75	
	Noon	SSE.	8	29.97	69	76	Latitude 32° 30′ N., longitude 77° 17′ W. Between noon and 4 p. m. wind shifted from SSE. to S. and SW., force 9.
	4 p. m.	SW.	9	29.85	68	72	
	8 p. m.	NW.	9	29.82	68	74	Wind shifted in a heavy rain squall at 5 p. m.
	10 p. m.	NW.	10	......	......	......	
	Midnight	NW.	10	29.73	58	75	

American steam-ship Knickerbocker, Captain Kemble—Continued.

Date.	Hour.	Wind.		Barometer.	Temperature.		Remarks.
					Air.	Water.	
Mar. 12	[illegible] a. m.	NNW.	9	29.41	54	55	
	8 a. m.	NNW.	9	29.51	44	45	Sea swell still heavy, but decreasing slightly.
	Noon	NNW.	8	29.60	43	45	Latitude 35° 28' N., longitude 74° 36' W. Weather fine and clear, sea still heavy.
	4 p. m.	NNW.	6	29.59	40	43	Sea rough, shipping much water.
	8 p. m.	NNW.	6	29.64	39	43	
	Midnight	NNW.	7	29.59	36	36	Weather boisterous, sea much very heavy; frequent snow squalls; ship all iced up.
Mar. 13	4 a. m.	NW.	8	29.64	30	30	
	8 a. m.	NW.	8	29.69	27	34	
	Noon	NW. by W.	8	29.71	24	34	Latitude 37° 24' N., longitude 75° 30' W. Heavy snow squalls.
	4 p. m.	NW.	8	29.74	24	36	
	8 p. m.	NW.	6	29.75	26	34	
	Midnight	NW.	8	29.64	25	35	Passed Scotland Light-ship at 4.15 a. m., March 14.

British bark Lady Lisgar, Captain Thomas.

March 12-18.—In about latitude 40° 30' N., longitude 55° W., encountered a heavy easterly gale; ship **straining and** making much water; lay to for several days and had to jettison part of cargo to save ship.

American Schooner **Lida Fowler**, *Captain Higgins.*

During the 12th, light airs from E. with a heavy NE. swell; high barometer; noon **position, latitude 36° 05' N.,** longitude 69° W. Towards evening, falling barometer, **with** increasing southeasterly **breeze, which by midnight** became a gale. About noon of the 12th, in latitude 37° 30' N., longitude 71° W., **the wind, which was blowing with** hurricane force from SE., **shifted** instantly **to** SW., with **snow** and hail, **and at 2 p. m. to W., with lowest barometer** 29.12. Towards midnight **it** moderated a **little and** the **barometer rose, and during the forenoon of the 12th the wind** died out somewhat, with occasional snow squalls, and **then increased to a moderate NW. gale. Position at noon, March** 13, latitude 38° N., longitude 70° 10' W. During the **forenoon of the 14th, light breeze from NNW., barometer 29.79,** and by midnight a strong gale again from NNW., **which lasted during the 15th, when it cleared up, with rising glass** and fine weather.

British steam-ship Lord [illegible], Captain Urquhart.

Date.	Hour.	Wind.		Barometer.	Temperature.		Remarks.
					Air.	Water.	
Mar. 11	Noon	[illegible]	2	[illegible]	46	52	Latitude 38° 51' N., longitude 66° 30' W.
	[illegible]	SW. by S.	2	29.29	44	52	
	4 p. m.	SW. by W.	2	29.24	42	50	Overcast.
	[illegible]	[illegible]	3	[illegible]	41	49	
	8 p. m.	[illegible]	4	29.10	43	50	Overcast.
	10 p. m.	[illegible]		29.19	[illegible]	50	
	Midnight	E. by S.	6	29.10	[illegible]	52	Cloudy.
Mar. 12	2 a. m.	ESE.	6	29.04	49	49	Wind increasing, with threatening appearance to SW.
	[illegible]	ESE.	[illegible]	29.24	50	52	Wind still increasing, with heavy rain.
	[illegible]	ESE.	[illegible]	29.34	54	54	Weather the same.
	8 a. m.	ESE.	[illegible]	29.42	54	54	Moderating a little with heavy rain.
	8.30 a. m.						Weather clearing.
	[illegible]						Wind suddenly shifted to NW., blowing a whole gale.

British steam-ship Lord Clive, Captain Urquhart—Continued.

Date.	Hour.	Wind.		Barometer.	Temperature.		Remarks.
					Air.	Water.	
Mar. 12	9.30 a. m.	....		....	....	....	Wind shifted suddenly to NW., blowing a complete hurricane, with violent squalls of wind, accompanied by hail and sleet.
	10 a. m.	NW.	12	29.18	....	....	Lowest temperature of air 50°. Assumed position, latitude 39° 19′ N., longitude 72° 40′ W.
	Noon	NW.	12	29.34	26	....	A complete hurricane, with tremendous sea and terrific squalls, accompanied by heavy snow. Latitude 39° 14′ N., longitude 72° 30′ W.
	2 p. m.	NW. by W.	12	29.34	26	....	Weather the same.
	4 p. m.	NW. by W.	12	29.44	26	....	Weather same.
	6 p. m.	NW.		29.50	26	....	Storm moderating, but still heavy squalls and much snow.
	8 p. m.	NW.		29.50	24	....	Wind and weather same.
	10 p. m.	WNW.		29.49	25	....	
	Midnight	....		29.54	21	....	Wind and weather same.
Mar. 13	2 a. m.	NW.	9	29.54	19	28	Strong gale with heavy squalls, accompanied by sleet and snow.
	4 a. m.	NW.	9	29.46	17	27	Assumed position, latitude 38° 50′ N., longitude 73° 50′ W.
	6 a. m.	NW.	9	29.46	18	27	
	8 a. m.	NW.	9	29.54	18	26	
	10 a. m.	NW.	9	29.54	18	26	
	Noon	NW.	9	29.55	20	26	Latitude 38° 40′ N., longitude 72° W.
	3 p. m.	NW.	8	29.54	18	26	
	5 p. m.	NW.	8	29.54	18	26	
	7 p. m.	NW.	9	29.64	19	24	
	Midnight.	NW.	9	29.64	18	24	High sea and much snow.
Mar. 14	2 a. m.	NW.	9	29.62	18	....	
	6 a. m.	NW.	9	29.69	22	....	
	8 a. m.	NW.	8	29.74	20	....	
	Noon	NW.	8	29.78	20	....	Fresh gale, with heavy squalls; sea moderate; came to anchor off the breakwater.

British steam-ship **Lydian** *Monarch, Capt. T. C. Haggett.*

***March* 11.**—**Gale set in** from NE., shifting to **E., force** 11; barometer 29.65.
***March* 13.**—**Gale set in from** SW., shifting **to SE., S.,** and SW., force 11. 5 p. m.: Latitude 40° 30′ N., longitude 65° 50 W.; barometer 29.05.

British *steam-ship Madura, Captain Doyle.*

(Liverpool to Portland, Me.)

***March* 11.**—7 **a. m.:** Latitude 50° 17′ N., longitude 51° 40′ W.; wind NE., 5; barometer 29.12; stormy and rainy.
***March* 12.**—7 **a.** m.: Latitude 41° 23′ N., longitude 56° 17′ W.; wind E., 4.; barometer 29.01,; stormy and rainy, **and wind** shifting, with violent squalls.
March 13.—7 a. m.: Latitude 42° N., longitude 60° 20′ W.; wind NW., 10; barometer 29.55; moderating a little.
March 14.—7 a. m.: Latitude 42° 34′ N., longitude 65° 19′ W.; wind NE., 6; barometer **29.51**; changeable and foggy.

American schooner *Messenger, Captain Falker.*

***March* 11.**—**Position at noon, latitude 36° 37′** N., longitude 74° 22′ W.; wind SE., 7.
***March* 12.—Wind backed to NW., 8 to 9.**
***March* 13.—Wind NW., 11, until** midnight, then moderating; lowest recorded barometer 28.91; **time and** position not **stated.**
***March* 14.—In latitude 37° 34′ N.,** longitude 72° 9′ W.; **wind N. to NNW., 8 to 9.**
***March* 15.—In latitude 37° 18′ N.,** longitude 73° 36′ W.; **wind NNW., 9, then moderating.**

American schooner Nantasket, Capt. E. A. Richardson.

March 11, 12, before and during which barometer only fell to 29.50 (correct). But for the first twelve hours and for nearly twenty-four hours it was nearly the same, vibrating .13, the most remarkable vibrations that I ever saw in a barometer. Its lowest reading, 29.50, was at 10 p. m. on the 11th, in latitude 37° N., longitude 74° 30′ W. Wind (highest) velocity of 100 miles per hour.

British steam-ship Nessmore, Captain Elliott.

March 11.—Gale set in from ENE.

March 12.—Between 7 p. m. and 9 p. m. of the 12th. About twelve hours before shifting into NW., the wind was shifting suddenly in fierce squalls, attended by heavy rain, into the S., SE., SW., and WSW., with raging cross-sea from every point of the compass; although the captain put the ship's head from one point to another all around to prevent her rolling so furiously, yet his attempts were futile, as whichever way her head was she was in a trough and remained so for some time, until the sea abated somewhat, owing to a heavy downpour of rain and the wind shifting suddenly to NW.

March 13.—11 a. m.: Latitude 39° 48′ N., longitude 60° 45′ W.; barometer (lowest) 29.10; moderated from E.; highest force, 11.

March 16.—A gale set in from SW., highest force 10, shifting to W. and NW. 3.55 p. m.: Latitude 42° 43′ N., longitude 43° 31′ W.; barometer (lowest) 28.73. Midnight: Moderated.

American brig Nettie, Captain Lowry.

March 11.—Latitude 39° 10′ N., longitude 73° 10′ W.; wind SE., force 7 to 8.

March 12.—Latitude 39° 22′ N., longitude 73° 5′ W.; wind backed from SE. to NE., force 9, and from that time increased to hurricane, backing to NW.

March 13.—Latitude 39° 32′ N., longitude 71° 33′ W.; wind NW., force 10, and moderating.

British bark Nora Wiggins, Captain Lawrence.

(Report communicated by Mr. Collins, first mate.)

At noon of the 10th, in latitude 38° 20′ N., longitude 56° W., the barometer read 29.67, falling rapidly; moderate breeze and heavy ground-swell from ENE. (The corrected reading of this vessel's barometer at this place and time is considerably too low, and, unless her reported position is considerably out, it throws a doubt upon the report of very low barometer the evening of the 12th, when the reading, corrected and reduced to mean sea level, was 28.37, the lowest reported by any vessel that encountered the hurricane off the coast. The barometer was an aneroid, and every effort was made by the New York Branch Hydrographic Office to verify the observation, the instrument having been compared with standard as soon as the vessel reached port. On April 2 the barometer was .77 high, and on the 14th .84 high, showing such a decided difference that the reported low reading of the 12th can not be regarded as trustworthy, especially in view of the rough usage she met with in the hurricane.)

On the 10th the barometer was falling rapidly, with a moderate breeze and heavy ground-swell from ENE. The next day about the same, but with heavy, dark banks of clouds to the north and south. By midnight the wind backed ESE., with rain, increasing during the forenoon of the 12th to a gale with heavy rain and sea; barometer very unsteady. About 6 p. m. the wind shifted very suddenly, after moderating about 15 minutes, to the south, gradually veering toward the west, and at 8 p. m. was blowing a hurricane from WSW., with heavy sea and blinding snow. A heavy sea struck the vessel on the starboard bow, crushing bulwarks, breaking thirteen stanchions, throwing the vessel on her beam ends, and flooding the forward deck-houses. During the remainder of the night, and up to 6 a. m. of the 13th, the barometer was very low and unsteady, fluctuating from 28.37 to 28.67, and then rising slowly. Heavy gale from W. and WNW., with snow, followed by clearing weather.

British brig Olive Branch, Captain Manthorn.

March 10.—Latitude 37° 10′ N., longitude 68° 4′ W.; wind NW. to N., 9; barometer steady at 30.24 throughout the day.

March 11.—Latitude 37° 53′ N., longitude 69° 7′ W.; wind N. by E. to NE., 9; barometer steady at 30.25.

March 12.—Latitude 38° 47′ N., longitude 71° 7′ W.; wind SE., 10; barometer 29.25.

March 13.—Latitude 39° 20′ N., longitude 70° 0′ W.; wind SE., 10; at 3 p. m. sudden shift to W., 12; barometer 29.05. Frequent squalls, with heavy snow.

March 14.—Wind W., 10; moderating and barometer rising; heavy snow.

British bark Patagonia, Captain Hibbert.

From March 9, in latitude 37° 22′ N., longitude 66° 45′ W., to March 14, latitude 39° 30′ N., longitude 68° 16′ W., continued succession of strong gales, commencing at NW., veering on the 11th to SE., and on the 12th to SW. and W. Gale continued to 15th, in latitude 39° 38′ N., longitude 67° 23′ W., veering to NNE., 9, and moderating. Lowest barometer March 13, 29.02, in latitude 39° 38′ N., longitude 68° 20′ W.

Norwegian bark Rosenberg, Captain Johannessen.

March 11.—Latitude 31° 59′ N., longitude 70° 14′ W. Experienced a severe electric storm. St. Elmo's fire on trucks and yard-arms. Sea full of phosphorescence. Wind SSE., 7 to 8, backing to SE., 9, then moderating for a few hours.

March 12.—Wind increasing to a strong gale and veering to NW., 9 to 10 (this probably about 1 a. m., in latitude 33° 30′ N., longitude 69° 30′ W.).

March 13.—Wind NW., 11, throughout the day.

March 14.—Wind NW. to NNW., 10 to 9.

March 15.—Wind NNW., 8 to 10, with squalls of hurricane force.

March 16.—8 a. m.: Moderated; latitude 34° 37′ N., longitude 68° 4′ W.

British steam-ship Samana, Captain Bermpohl.

March 11.—Noon: Latitude 30° 1′ N., longitude 74° W.; wind S. by E., 6 to 8; cloudy. 2 p. m.: Wind SSE., 8; threatening weather; wind continued same in direction, increasing in force to 9, until midnight; wind shifted suddenly to NW. and increased in force to 10, with squally, threatening weather; latitude 31° 30′ N., longitude 73° 30′ W.

March 12.—2 a. m.: Wind NW. by N., 10 to 11, continuing the same in force and direction throughout the day. Noon: Latitude 32° 3′ N., longitude 74° 17′ W. Midnight: Wind backed to NW. and moderated to force 8.

March 13.—2 a. m.: Wind NW., 8 to 7; threatening weather. 8 a. m.: Wind WNW., 8, continuing same in force until noon. Noon: Latitude 33° 1′ N., longitude 74° 39′ W.; wind increased in force to 11, with violent squalls; cloudy threatening weather. 3 p. m.: wind shifted to W. by N., 11. 6 p. m.: Wind NW., 11. 8 p. m.: Wind W., 11 to 10; weather threatening and squally.

March 14.—2 a. m.: Wind W., 10; barometer 29.38. 7 a. m.: Wind NW., 10; barometer 29.48. Noon: Latitude 33° 56′ N., longitude 71° 30′ W.; wind NW., 10; barometer 29.54. 4 p. m.: Wind NNW., 10; barometer 29.56; wind same until midnight, with violent squalls. Midnight: Barometer 29.78.

March 15.—2 a. m.: Wind N. by W., 10; barometer 29.78. 4 a. m.: wind N. by W., 9; barometer 29.86. Noon: Latitude 35° 26′ N., longitude 72° 10′ W.; moderate gale from N. by W.

American bark Samuel B. Hale, Captain Haves.

March 11.—Latitude at noon, 32° 10′ N., longitude 68° 40′ W.; wind SE., 7.

March 12.—Wind N. by W. to NW. to NE., 8 to 9. Assumed position at noon, latitude 33° N., longitude 69° W.

March 13.—Wind NE., 9 to 11. Assumed position at noon, latitude 33° 40′ N., longitude 69° 30′ W.

March 14.—Wind NE., 9 to 11. Assumed position at noon, latitude 34° 10′ N., longitude 69° 40′ W.

March 15.—Wind NW., 7. Assumed position at noon, latitude 34° 40′ N., longitude 69° 30′ W.

March 16.—Position at noon, latitude 34° 55′ N., longitude 68° 56′ W. Wind N., 7 to 6, and moderated.

Norwegian bark Saranak, Captain Morthensen.

March 10.—4 a. m.: Latitude 36° 35′ N., longitude 71° 38′ W.; wind NNE., 7; barometer 30.19.

March 13.—4 p. m.: Latitude 37° 16′ N., longitude 70° 29′ W.; wind W., 10; ran before the wind; barometer 29.44.

March 15.—8 a. m.: Latitude 38° 27′ N., longitude 65° 53′ W.; wind SW., with heavy squalls from S.; barometer 29.60.

March 16.—Noon: Latitude 38° 21′ N., longitude 65° 40′ W.; wind NNW.; barometer 29.65.

March 17.—Noon: Latitude 38° 02′ N., longitude 69° 09′ W.; wind NW.; barometer 29.82.

During this storm the wind shifted as follows: NNE., E., SE., S., W., SW., S., SW., W., NW., NNW. The weather continued unsettled and variable until the 22d. Wind shifting from S., SE., SW., and N., with heavy squalls and rain.

British steam-ship Serapis, Captain Dobson.

Date.	Hour.	Wind.		Barom-eter.	Sea.	Remarks.
Mar. 11	4 a. m.	NE.	5	30.22	Mod. NE.	Clear.
	8 a. m.	NE.	5	30.22	Mod. NE.	Clear.
	Noon	ENE.	5	30.15	Mod. NE.	Clear. Latitude 38° 41′ N., longitude 71° 19′ W.
	4 p. m.	ENE.	6	30.10	Strong ENE.	Slightly overcast. About 4 p. m., in about latitude 38° N., longitude 71° 40′ W., a bank of heavy, thick, black, inky clouds to SW.
	8 p. m.	ENE.	6	30.00	Strong ENE.	Misty, with rain.
	Midnight	ENE.	6	29.90	Strong ENE.	Misty, with rain.
Mar. 12	2 a. m.	ENE.	6	29.85	Strong ENE.	Misty, with rain.
	4 a. m.	ENE.	6	29.75	Strong ENE.	Misty, with rain.

British steam-ship Serapis, Captain Dobson—Continued.

Date.	Hour.	Wind.		Barometer.	Sea.	Remarks.
Mar. 12	5 a.m.	N.	8	[illegible]	Strong ENE.	Weather same. Between 5 and 6 a.m. the wind shifted suddenly in a squall from ENE. to NW.; there was no backing or veering and the change took place without any interval of calm.
	6 a.m.	NW.	12	29.[illegible]	Heavy NW.	Thick snow; continued blowing a hurricane, with thick snow and heavy NW. sea, until noon on the 13th.
	8 a.m.	NW.	12	29.[illegible]	....	
	9 a.m.	NW.	12	29.[illegible]	....	
	10 a.m.	NW.	12	29.45	....	
	11 a.m.	NW.	12	29.[illegible]	....	
	Noon	NW.	12	29.41	....	Latitude 40° N., longitude [illegible]° 12′ W.
	2 p.m.	NW.	12	29.39	....	
	4 p.m.	NW.	12	29.[illegible]	....	
	6 p.m.	NW.	12	29.[illegible]	....	
	8 p.m.	NW.	12	29.[illegible]	....	
	10 p.m.	NW.	12	29.[illegible]	....	
	Midnight	NW.	12	29.[illegible]	....	
Mar. 13	2 a.m.	NW.	12	29.[illegible]	....	
	4 a.m.	NW.	12	29.[illegible]	....	
	8 a.m.	NW.	12	29.[illegible]	....	
	Noon	NW.	11	29.[illegible]	....	Moderating; position by dead reckoning, latitude [illegible]° [illegible]′ N., longitude [illegible]° [illegible]′ W.
	4 p.m.	NW.	9	29.[illegible]	....	
	6 p.m.	....		29.[illegible]	....	
	7 p.m.	NW.	8	29.[illegible]	....	After this barometer rose rapidly; gale moderated.

British steam-ship **Stockholm City, Captain** *Thompson.*

March 13.—Gale set in from E. by N., ending same day with **wind S.; highest force of wind, 11. At 10 p. m., in latitude** [illegible]° [illegible]′ N., longitude [illegible]° [illegible]′ W.; barometer [illegible] **(lowest).**

British steam-ship St. Ronans, Capt. H. Campbell.

March 12.—Gale set in from NE. 1 a. m.: Latitude 41° 32′ N., longitude 51° 12′ W.; wind NNE., force 9; barometer 29.50.

March 13.—Wind SE., thence to NW., force 9. 11 a. m.: Latitude 41° 3′ N., longitude 58° 59′ W.; barometer 29.38.

March 14.—Wind N. to WNW.; latitude 40° 53′ N., longitude 60° 26′ W.; barometer 29.50. Moderated.

British steam-ship Switzerland, Captain Ueberweg.

March 12.—Noon: Gale set in from SE., shifting to WSW.; highest force 8. 6.45 p. m.: Latitude 39° N., longitude 65° W.; barometer 29.50.

March 13.—Noon: Gale abated.

American bark Wakefield, Captain Crowell.

(Voyage from Pernambuco to New York.)

March 11.—Noon position, latitude [illegible]° [illegible]′ **N., longitude 63° W.;** cloudy weather**; moderate** breezes; long, rolling swell **from** NW. All sail set.

March 12.—Noon position, latitude [illegible]° 12′ N., longitude **64° 50′ W.** From 4 p.m. to midnight: Wind backing to SE. and then to southward; continues clear and pleasant; wind freshening; sea smooth; all sail set; barometer [illegible] at midnight.

March 13.—From midnight to 8 a.m.: Clear and pleasant; all sail set; sea smooth, but wind increasing rapidly from SW.; barometer [illegible] at 8 a.m. Noon position, latitude [illegible]° [illegible]′ N., longitude [illegible]° [illegible]′ W. From 8 a.m. to 4 p.m. Cloudy, with a passing shower; wind and sea rapidly increasing; took in light sails; barometer [illegible] at 4 p.m. **From** 4 p.m. to midnight: Wind SW. and increasing; took in top-gallant sails; at 7 p.m. took in mainsail, **spanker,** and flying jib; at 8 p.m. wind suddenly changed to NNW. in heavy squall of wind and rain; barometer **29.92 at midnight.**

March 14.—From midnight to 8 a. m.: Cloudy, and strong breezes from W. by N.; sea rough and heavy swells; at 4 a. m. set main-top-gallant sail and mainsail; at 8 a. m. tacked ship to SW.; barometer 29.87. Noon position, latitude 27° 32′ N., longitude 65° 54′ W. From 8 a. m. to 4 p. m.: At noon tacked ship to northward; wind backing to westward; heavy swell from westward; barometer 29.87 at 4 p. m. From 4 p. m. to midnight: Wind increasing; at 8 p. m. took in mainsail; weather windy looking.

March 15.—From midnight until 8 a. m.: Cloudy and squally; wind W. and sea increasing; reduced ship down to reefed top-sails, reefed foresail, mizzen-stay sail, and foretop-mast stay-sail; at 8 a. m. wore ship around on starboard tack; barometer 29.77. Noon position, latitude 27° 18′ N., longitude 65° 50′ W. From 8 a. m. to 4 p. m.: Cloudy, with heavy squalls making in NW.; took in upper foresail and furled it; sea heavy, broken, and irregular. From 4 p. m. until midnight: Wind WNW.; continuous heavy squalls of wind and rain; sea very heavy and irregular; ship laboring and rolling badly; barometer 29.72 at midnight.

March 16.—From midnight until 8 a. m.: Blowing furiously from NW., with squalls and heavy rain; sea heavy, with heavy combers; ship laboring badly and shipping large quantities of water; barometer 29.82 at 8 a. m. Noon position, latitude 26° 34′ N., longitude 66° 40′ W. From 8 a. m. to 4 p. m.: Continues same, but sea not so bad; wind NNW.; set upper foretop-sail, reefed. From 4 p. m. to midnight: Gradually moderating and the sea going down; took reef out of upper main-topsail and foresail; barometer 29.92 at midnight.

German steam-ship Wandrahm, Captain Rehse.

March 13.—Gale set in from E. by S., shifting to E. by N.; highest force 10. 11 a. m.: Latitude 44° 29′ N., longitude 63° 20′ W.; barometer 29.67 (correct). Captain Rehse reports further as follows: On the 13th, 4 p. m., must have been close to Sambro, but too thick to see anything; kept the ship outside till next afternoon. It blew very heavy that night, with thick rain, hail, and snow, and very heavy sea. I received no damage, and got in all right on the 14th, afternoon.

British ship Warrior, Captain Kitchen.

From March 12, in latitude 42° 36′ N., longitude 69° 40′ W., to March 17, in latitude 42° 52′ N., longitude 69° 4′ W., a succession of strong gales, commencing at ESE., veering to E. by N. to N., and on the 16th to WNW. Lowest recorded barometer reading was 29.37, on March 13, in latitude 42° 4′ N., longitude 69° 4′ W.

German steam-ship Werra, Captain Bussius.

March 12.—Wind SE., force 6.
March 13.—11 a. m.: Latitude 40° 20′ N., longitude 69° 25′ W.; bar. 29.25; gale shifted from SE. to S., SW., and W.

Belgian steam-ship Westernland, Captain Randle.

March 12.—Latitude 40° 44′ N., longitude 59° 1′; wind, ESE., 10. At 5.55 p. m. barometer read 29.35 (lowest); shifts of wind, E. by S., SE., S.
March 13.—Wind S.; gale moderated.

Norwegian bark Wilhelm Birkedal, Captain Stangebye.

Date.	Hour.	Wind.	Barometer.	Remarks.
Mar. 11	Noon	SE.	....	Wind increasing, with falling barometer and rain. Latitude 34° 11′ N., longitude 74° 25′ W.
	8 p. m.....	SE. 10	29.79	Vessel under two lower top-sails only. From 8 until 11.30 p. m. wind and weather the same, heavy head-sea making; indications of a shift of wind.
	11.30 p. m	....	....	Wind shifted suddenly to northwest with heavy squalls of rain and great change in temperature. Wind not so strong as it shifted, but increasing in force towards the morning, blowing very hard from NW. and WNW., and continuing the same throughout the day, March 12th.
Mar. 12	Noon	....	....	Latitude 35° 57′ N., longitude 73° 22′ W. barometer 28.64, lowest (time not given.)
Mar. 13	....	....	....	Wind more moderate but still strong and shifting a little more to the northward. Heavy snow squalls both on 12th and 13th. Sea moderating.

This vessel's barometer was mercurial, kept in cabin 16 feet above sea-level. It was compared with standard at the New York Branch Hydrographic Office, March 2d, when its error was .023 too high, and this error has been used in correcting the observed readings. The corrected readings, however, are very low, and do not agree with other data. From the vessel's position on the 11th, it is evident, by comparison of her barometer readings with those of other vessels in the vicinity, that there is some error not accounted for, and this throws doubt upon the reported low reading on the 12th. On April 26 her barometer read .101 high of standard.

Pilot-boat William H. Starbuck, of New York.

(Report communicated by Pilot Heath.)

[Note.—Barometer aneroid, said to be correct, but no comparison obtained with standard.]

March 11.—Noon: The *William H. Starbuck* was 10 miles S. from Barnegat, about 8 miles off shore; wind ENE., fresh breeze, hazy, with light rain; barometer 30. 4 p. m.: Wind hauled to ESE., blowing fresh breeze; light rain and hazy; stood off shore, heading ENE. 6 p. m.: Was about 18 miles ESE. from Barnegat, wind ESE., having increased in force to strong breeze; barometer 30; hove to, being far enough off shore.

March 12.—1 a. m.: Wind N., blowing a gale and squalls; ugly, squally weather, accompanied by hail and rain; glass had fallen but a very little; headed in W. by S. until soundings were obtained in 10 fathoms, about 8 miles from shore. 4 a. m.: Wind N., blowing heavy squalls; wore around and hove to on port tack. 6 a. m.: Wind NNW., blowing heavy gale, with terrific squalls; snowing hard, and could see nothing; heavy sea, spray flying, decks deluged with water; got out drags and put out oil-bags on weather-side, five bags strung along the side. Sea would strike drags or sea anchor, and then come alongside perfectly harmless on account of meeting drag and oil slick. 4 p. m.: About this time had worst of storm; wind blowing a perfect hurricane from WNW.; the only things that kept the vessel up were the sea anchor and oil bags; at this time the barometer was 29.70, jumping at least .1 each way; had drifted so that we judged our position to be about 18 or 20 miles east from Barnegat. About 11 p. m., while still blowing a gale from NNW., collided with the steamship *Japanese*. After this engaged in clearing wreck. Wind remained NNW., blowing a gale, moderating at times, till the 14th; snowing steadily all this time.

March 13.—Midnight: Glass commenced to rise.

March 15.—Got first observations since storm set in, and found vessel to be in latitude 39° 31′ N., longitude 73° W.

GREENWICH NOON OBSERVATIONS.

The following list gives a brief synopsis of marine data used in the preparation of the accompanying daily charts. Each wind arrow corresponds to an observation recorded in these columns, and can be referred to, in any case, by using as co-ordinates the date of the chart and the latitude and longitude of the center of the arrow. Land data are from the daily weather maps published by the U. S. Signal Service. In a few cases data have been obtained by interpolation from journals, storm reports, etc., in order to cover areas from which no other data are as yet at hand, but in every such case it is so stated in a foot note. Barometer readings are in all cases corrected by last comparison with standards at the various branch hydrographic offices (referred to the Kew standard), and reduced to 32° F. and mean sea level. Readings of a mercurial barometer are followed by the letter *m*; aneroid, *a*.

In preparing the four daily charts of the area under consideration, material assistance has been obtained from observations of vessels beyond the actual limits of the area charted. It is only practicable at the present time, however, to publish the observations taken on board vessels within the limits of the charts (lat. 25° to 50° N., long. 50° to 85° W.), and these only in brief.

The symbols used in the various columns are explained as follows:

Wind.

Beaufort's scale.	Miles per hour.	Metres per second.
0. Calm	2	0.9
1. Light air	5	2.2
2. Light breeze	[illegible]	4.5
3. Gentle breeze	15	6.7
4. Moderate breeze	20	8.9
5. Fresh breeze	25	11.0
6. Strong breeze	35	15.6
7. Moderate gale	42	18.7
8. Fresh gale	50	22.3
9. Strong gale	60	26.7
10. Whole gale	70	31.2
11. Storm	80	35.7
12. Hurricane	90	40.2

Weather.*

b. Clear blue sky.
c. Cloudy weather.
d. Drizzling, or light rain.
f. Fog, or foggy weather.
g. Gloomy, or dark, stormy looking weather.
h. Hail.
l. Lightning.
m. Misty weather.
o. Overcast.
p. Passing showers of rain.
q. Squally weather.
r. Rainy weather, or continuous rain.
s. Snow, snowy weather, or snow falling.
t. Thunder.
u. Ugly appearances, or threatening weather.
v. Variable weather.
w. Wet, or heavy dew.
z. Hazy.

Sea.

B. Broken or irregular sea.
C. Chopping, short, or cross sea.
G. Ground swell.
H. Heavy sea.
L. Long rolling sea.
M. Moderate sea or swell.
R. Rough sea.
S. Smooth sea.
T. Tide-rips.

* To indicate greater intensity the letter is underlined thus: r, heavy rain; r, very heavy rain, etc.

March 11, 1888.

Vessel.	Master.	Position.		Wind.		Barometer.	Temp. of air (Fahr.)	Weather by symbols.	Remarks.
		Lat. N.	Long. W.	Direction, true.	Force, Beaufort.				
		° ′	° ′				°		
A. D. Bache	Lt. Mason, U. S. N.	35 08	81 11	NE.	6	30.04 a.	71	o. c. q.	Squally and rainy. Cross sea from SSE.
Ailsa	Evans	22 23	74 09	E.	4	30.16 m.	64	c.	Clouds SE. and E. Sea L. from N. Fine weather.
Alsatia	Murray	41 [illegible]	58 08	NE.	2	30.04 m.	35	....	Mod. E'ly sea; clouds from W.
Andes	Chabrol	37 45	73 42	SE.	4	30.13 a.	44	o. c.	Mod. SE. sea.
Anna	Menkens	39 42	58 15	ENE.	9	29.50 m.	[illegible]	q. r.	Very high cross sea from ENE.
Baltimore	Tremery	41 35	54 56	ENE.	8	29.91 m.	48	o. c.	Clouds ENE. Sea H. from ENE.
Barracouta	Hubbard	23 28	68 36	ENE.	4	29.91 a.	67	c.	Mod. ENE. wind and sea. Cloudy at times.
Bengore Head	Beady	37 41	65 38	N.	8	29.99 m.	51	c.	Wind veered to ESE. at mid. L. H. sea from NE.
Bohemia	Kandell	40 38	70 18	E'ly.	7	30.40 a.	34	o. c.	Clouds and S. sea from E. Winds variable.
Brooklyn City	Pitt	46 23	60 52	E.	4	30.39 a.	24	b. c.	Clouds and L. H. sea from E.
Bulgarian	Perry	43 17	65 18	ENE.	3	30.36 m.	40	b. c.	Clouds S. Fine weather.
Caribbean*	Dinsdale	30 10	67 40	NE.	2	30.12 m.	....	....	Somewhat cloudy. Long NE. swell.
Carthaginian	MacNichol	42 40	57 00	ESE.	5	30.61 m.	32	o. p.	H. SE. sea. Fresh breeze snow and hail past 24 hrs.
Catania	Franck	35 40	69 30	SSE.	2	30.32 a.	....	o. u.	Long mod. sea from SSE. Calm at midnight.
City of Augusta	Catharine	37 30	74 25	SE.	8	30.14 a.	45	c. u.	More rain. Mod. SE. sea.
City of Chester	Lewis	40 27	74 03	E. by N.	8	30.43 a.	37	o. r.	Clouds ENE. Sea H. from E. by N.
City of San Antonio	Wilder	31 00	78 11	SE.	4	30.07 a.	64	c. r.	Mod. SE. sea.
Colon	Henderson	28 00	74 02	ESE.	4	30.25 a.	68	c.	Heavy clouds and mod. sea from SE.
Dora	Meyer	38 22	65 43	NE. by N.	[illegible]	30.20 m.	56	o. c.	Heavy storm; high, wild sea past day.
Edam	van der Zee	43 06	72 03	E.	5	30.38 m.	34	b. c.	Clouds and mod. sea from E.
Edward E. Barrett*	Hughes	40 55	67 20	E. by N.	4	29.38 a.	....	....	Clear, fine weather. Light to mod. NE. and ENE. winds.
Egypt	Sommer	41 34	53 00	ENE.	2	29.87 a.	40	o. c.	Clouds and H. sea from ENE.
Elbe	Meyer	40 22	69 35	E.	3	30.33 m.	37	b. c.	Fair weather; Lt. S'ly and E'ly winds past 24 hrs.
Forfrelander	Bruns	24 05	74 30	E.	4	30.20 a.	74	o. c.	Clouds E. and SSE. Sea L. from NNE.
Furnessia	Hedderwick	45 14	29 55	N.	10	29.43 a.	31	g. q. s. n.	Fine and clear; wind falling during past 24 hrs.
Glenburn*	Johnston	22 40	58 09	N.W. by W.	4	29.93 m.	....	q.	Mod. to strong gale with squalls during past 24 hrs.
Istrian	Fox	42 02	56 22	NE.	8	29.11 m.	43	c. n.	Strong gale throughout. Wind backed two points.
Jane Adeline	Oates	Vineyard Haven		ESE.	2	30.28 a.	....	z.	Threatening sky.
Julia	Vieira	25 05	55 47	SE.	3	30.17 m.	77	b. c.	Clouds and broken sea from SE.
Kennett	Crask	33 27	73 00	ESE.	7	30.16 a.	50	o. c.	Clouds SW. Sea L. from ESE.
Knickerbocker	Kemble	31 47	77 12	SE.	7	29.95 m.	74	o. r. q.	All elements increasing. Sea H. H. from SE. and SSW.
Lake Superior	Stewart	41 11	65 00	NE.	4	30.22 m.	35	c.	Clouds ENE. Sea H. from NE.
La Gascogne	Santelli	40 40	73 10	E.	3	30.25 a.	40	b. c.	Overcast after 4 a. m. Sea smooth.
La Normandie	de Kersabiec	40 25	67 32	NE.	5	30.23 m.	37	r. s.	Clouds NE. Sea H. from ENE.
Lord Clive	Urquhart	39 53	66 00	NE.	5	30.38 m.	40	c. m.	Strong NE. gale, mod. to 4 a. m., then mod. and fine weather.
Lord Gough	Hughes	38 40	61 41	NNE.	6	30.15 m.	50	c. q. c.	Clouds and L. sea from NE.
Lorenzo D. Baker	Wiley	35 00	72 00	E.	7	30.24 a.	62	c. c.	Clouds SE. sea L. from NNE. Weather mod. past 24 hrs.
Lucy W. Snow	Burgess	28 34	55 07	WNW.	6	30.09 a.	66	c.	Clouds NW. Sea L. from SSW.
Lydian Monarch	Haggett	40 35	55 40	NE.	11	29.94 m.	53	g. r.	Clouds and sea from N.
Manhattan	Stevens	33 37	79 45	S.	9	29.92 a.	64	o. g.	At 4 p. m. strong breeze from NNW.

* Data obtained by excerpts taken from journal or storm report.

March 11, 1888—Continued.

Vessel.	Master.	Position. Lat. N.	Long. W.	Wind. Direction, true.	Force, Beaufort.	Barometer.	Temp. of air (Fahr.).	Weather by symbols.	Remarks.
Nantucket*	Richardson	35 56	74 00	SE.	3	30.16 a.	......	c. g.	Wind veered NE. to SE. R. sea from ENE.
Nessmore	Elliott	38 12	66 42	NNE.	5	30.07 m.	47	c.	Wind variable and unsteady. Clouds NE. and NW.
New Orleans	Halsey	38 05	74 38	S.	6	30.33 a.	42	c. g.	Clouds and mod. sea from E.
Newport	Shackford	34 36	74 30	SE.	4	30.17 a.	63	c.	Pleasant and partly cloudy during the day.
Orinoco	Garvin	32 22	64 50	N.	7	30.41 a.	58	b. c.	Fine weather. Clouds from N. and NW.
Oxford	James	39 13	59 11	ENE.	10	28.91 a.	......	o. q. r.	N. clouds and H. sea from ENE.
Republic	Davison	41 12	50 05	ENE.	8	30.64 a.	38	b. c.	Continual sheet-lightning at SE. and E. R., E'ly sea.
Rio Grande	Lewis	27 05	80 10	SE. by S.	6	30.04 a.	63	o. c. r.	Clouds from SW. Mod. SE. and S. sea.
Samana	Bernpohl	28 40	73 10	ESE.	2	30.33 a.	......	o. c.	Clouds from E. L. sea from NNE.
Serapis*	Dobson	38 20	70 40	NE.	5	30.18 a.	......	......	Mod. gale to fresh breeze from NNW. to NE. Rain squalls first part, clearing afterwards.
State of Georgia	Moodie	41 22	54 30	NE. by N.	8	30.12 a.	40	c.	R., NE'ly sea. Mostly fair weather during the day.
State of Texas	Williams	34 15	76 35	SE.	6	30.27 a.	......	o.	Lt. N'ly winds veering to SE. at 6 a. m. R., SE. sea.
Switzerland	Ueberweg	39 40	57 07	NNE.	7	29.94 a.	50	p.	Clouds and sea from NE. Water-spout at 6.30 p. m.
The Queen	Heeley	41 30	48 50	NE.	6	30.17 a.	43	o. c.	Clouds and mod. sea from NE.
Thornhill	Wetherell	28 05	19 10	SE.	7	30.04 a.	74	o. q.	Fresh gales, rain, and squalls during night. Wind going S'd.
Trinidad	Fraser	39 26	72 54	ESE.	3	29.60 a.	45	g. o.	Clouds from N. Ground-swell from ESE.
Wandrahm	Rebse	43 26	22 00	NE.	7	30.17 a.	37	o. r.	Mod. gale and H. sea from NE.
Werra	Bussius	42 12	57 36	NE.	4	30.22 m.	43	b.	Clouds and heavy sea from NE.
Westernland	Randle	40 19	70 11	SE. by S.	5	30.25 m.	37	b.	Fine clear weather, L., E'ly sea.
Wyanoke	Boaz	40 00	74 00	ESE.	3	30.22 a.	61	o. r.	Clouds and C. sea from SE.

March 12, 1888.

Vessel.	Master.	Lat. N.	Long. W.	Wind direction.	Force.	Barometer.	Temp.	Weather.	Remarks.
Allen	Evans	32 44	74 05	WNW.	10	29.83 m.	49	o. c. q.	Terrific gale. Sea H. from NNW.
Andes	Clunkert	37 00	73 30	NW. by W.	11	30.19 a.	......	c. q.	Clouds NW. Sea H. from SSE.
Anna	Menkens	40 38	58 20	ENE.	7-8	30.12 m.	50	c. g.	Very high cross sea from NE.
Baltimore	Tremery	40 35	66 33	ENE.	5	30.13 m.	46	o. r.	Mod. ENE. sea.
Bangore Head	Brady	38 50	62 16	SE.	4	29.65 m.	57	b. c.	At 4 a. m., wind veered to SE., increasing. Midnight SSE. **gale**; lightning. Sea H.
Brooklyn City	Fitt	46 40	08 16	ESE.	5	29.74 a.	56	c. g.	Clouds ESE. **Sea R. H. from E. by S.**
Caribbean*	Daniel	34 15	64 00	SSE.	9	29.83 m.	......	......	Increasing wind and rain. At mid-night suddenly calm. Bar. 29.13.
Catania	Franck	29 03	66 07	S.	6-7	29.87 a.	69	**o. g.**	At 2 p. m. wind shifted to SE. and grew stronger.
City of Augusta	Catherine	**24 20**	76 30	NW.	10	29.93 a.	47	b.	Clear and cold. **Sea** from NW.
City of Chester	Lewis	**40 23**	67 00	E. by N.	8	29.72 a.	50	o. c.	Clouds ENE. **Sea H.** from E. by N.
City of Lincoln	Fry	**38 31**	58 20	NNW.	3	29.79 m.	......	b.	Light var. winds, showery past day.
City of San **Antonio**	Wilder	30 **10**	78 57	NNW.	**5**	29.89 a.	**44**	b. c.	Clouds **NW. Sea mod.** from NNW.
Colon	Henderson	34 **10**	73 50	NW.	**9**	29.83 a.	46	b. c.	Clouds **from NW.** Very H. C. sea.
Dora	Meyer	30 23	63 38	S. by **E.**	**8**	29.78 m.	77	**o. p.**	**Irregular winds;** confused sea **past day.**

* **Data obtained by interpolation from journal or storm report.**

March 12, 1888—**Continued.**

Vessel.	Master.	Position. Lat. N.	Position. Long. W.	Wind. Direction. (true).	Wind. Force. (Beaufort).	Barometer.	Temp. of air (Fahr.).	Weather by symbols.	Remarks.
		° ′	° ′	*			°		
Edward E. Barrett*	Hughes	40 30	63 30	E. by S.	5	29.79 a.			Clouding up; bar. falling; wind freshening from E. to E. by S.
Egypt	Summer	41 48	57 28	ENE.	9	30.10 a.	46	o. c.	Clouds from ENE. Sea H. from ENE.
Elbe	Meyer	41 [illegible]	61 30	E.	4	29.98 m.	45	c.	Fair. Cloudless at night; overcast in the morning.
Energy*		36 30	69 00	S. by W.	7	29.90 (a.)			Mod. S. to SSW. gale last part.
Fjordenheimdet	Broom	39 30	75 00	NNW.	8	29.90 a.	50	o. r.	Strong gale. Heavy rain during the night.
Formosa	Hedderwick	42 44	71 32	W. by N.	10	29.29 a.	25	s. q.	Heavy WNW. sea; terrific squalls.
Glenbern*	Johnsen	31 30	59 20	NWly.	9	29.42 m.		b.	Strong NW. gale and squally, followed by mod. weather.
Iceland	Fox	43 04	50 47	NE.	6	30.05 m.	45	o. g.	Fresh gale for 20 hours. Strong breeze last 4.
Julius	Vieira	27 33	73 41	NNW.	4	30.07 a.	68	d.	Broken sea from N. At times cloudy.
Kenmax	Gleig	41 54	32 07	NE.	5	29.95 m.	50	b.	Mod. NE. sea.
Kennett	Smith	39 00	74 30	N.	11	29.23 a.	30	s.	At 4 a. m. wind hauled to N.
Knickerbocker	Kemble	34 40	73 59	NNW.	9	29.72 m.	45	b. r.	Sea S. H. Gale shifted by the S. to NW. in a heavy squall.
Lake Superior	Stewart	45 08	50 04	E.	6	30.06 m.	32	o. c.	Fresh to strong winds all day. Clouds and H. sea from E.
Lampasas	Crowell	27 17	80 13	NE. [illegible]	3	30.04 a.	75	d.	Lt. rain during p. m.; clearing. At midnight gale from N.
La Normandie	de Kersabiec	43 36	51 12	E.	6	30.02 m.	40	s.	Heavy clouds from E. Sea H. from ENE.
Lida Fowler*	Higgins	35 00	70 30	SSE.	10	29.53 a.			At noon sudden shift to NW., and at 2 to W.; bar. 29.10.
Lord Clive	Urquhart	39 10	74 20	ESE.	8	29.30 m.	50	r. g. e. l.	Lightning from NW.; heavy rain.
Lord Gough	Hughes	38 05	77 22	NE.	4	29.97 m.	54	b. c. q.	Clouds from ENE. and E. Long sea from NE.
Lorenzo D. Baker	Wiley	29 14	72 40	NW.	10	29.51 a.	67	c. m.	Gale from SE., changing to NW. Stormy.
Lucy W. Snow	Margrave	32 40	58 43	WNW.	2	30.49 a.	66	o. c.	Clouds from S. Sea R. and irregular in direction.
Lydian Monarch	Haggett	44 34	61 29	E.	4	29.92 m.	30	c. g.	Clouds from E. Fine breeze during the day.
Manhattan	Stevens	38 44	80 00	NE. by N.	7	30.37 a.	59	b. c.	Clouds NE. Sea H. from ENE.
Nantucket	Richardson	37 00	75 00	NW.	11	29.38 a.		o. r. q.	At 10 p. m. the NE. gale jumped to a hurricane from NW.
Newcastle	Elliott	30 45	63 00	E.	3	30.22 m.	57	g.	Clouds NE. Heavy sea NE. Unsteady breeze during past 24 hours.
New Orleans	Halsey	34 30	74 29	NW.	9	30.00 a.	40	b.	Strong gale, shifting from E. to S. and to NW. Bar. 29.80.
Newport	Shackford	34 50	75 00	NW.	11	29.73 a.	45	o. m. q.	Clouds and heavy sea from NW.
Ortolan	Garvin	32 22	64 30	SSW.	4	29.81 a.	70	r. g.	Rain and bad weather past day.
Oxford	Jabra	40 25	50 10	ENE.	8	30.07 a.		c. o.	Clouds ENE. and SE. Very heavy ENE. sea.
Richmond Hill	Hyde	46 30	74 10	E.	7	29.41 m.	45	r.	Clouds and heavy sea from E.; incessant rain.
Regis	Karstens	43 31	56 12	NE. by E.	7	30.04 m.	33	o. c. q.	Clouds and sea NE'ly.
Sarnaen	Stoneposal	37 25	70 01	NW.	11	29.45 a.		b. c. o.	Rough, cross sea; blowing a gale during the day.
Scorpio*	Dolson	40 19	72 00	NW.	12	29.20 a.			Bar. falling steadily. Wind strong from 2 to 12 NE. and ENE. About 6 a. m. (G. T.) suddenly shifted to NW., blowing a hurricane.

* Data obtained by interpolation from journal or storm report.

March 12, 1888—Continued.

Vessel.	Master.	Position.		Wind.		Barometer.	Temp. of air (Fahr.).	Weather by symbols.	Remarks.
		Lat. N.	Long. W.	Direction true.	Force, Beaufort.				
State of Georgia	Moodie	° ′ 42 30	° ′ 61 45	NE.	5-6	30.11 a.	° 33	o. r.	Wind E. till mid.; force 10-5; then shifted to SW.
State of Texas	Williams	36 30	74 30	NW.	11	30.12 a.	......	o.	Strong SE. breeze veering to NNW. Heavy thunder and lightning.
Stockholm City	Thompson	42 30	68 43	E. ½ N.	7	29.92 a.	33	o. m. s.	Increasing breeze, cloudy, hazy weather.
St. Ronans	Campbell	41 22	52 40	NNE.	5	29.81 a.	48	c.	High NNE. sea. Rain, snow, and lightning during the day.
Switzerland	Ueberweg	39 00	62 30	SE.	8	30.11 a.	52	c. p.	Fresh NE. gale, mod. at 8 a. m., and hauling to SE.
The Queen	Heeley	41 06	65 10	E. by S.	6	29.74 a.	49	o. g.	Clouds from E. Mod. sea from ENE.
Thornhill	Wetherell	26 06	80 04	NW.	4	30.05 a.	68	b.	A. M., fresh gale and rain; clearing at noon; evening drizzling.
Wandrahm	Rehse	41 37	57 24	NE. by E.	6	30.23 a.	......	o. r. q.	Rough sea from E.
Werra	Bussius	34 09	60 42	ENE.	3	30.17 m.	41	c.	Clouds and mod. sea from ENE.
Westernland	Randle	42 27	64 57	E. by N.	5	29.84 m.	40	b. c.	Fresh to strong breezes; clear weather during the day.

March 13, 1888.

Vessel.	Master.	Lat. N.	Long. W.	Direction true.	Force, Beaufort.	Barometer.	Temp. of air (Fahr.).	Weather by symbols.	Remarks.
Aller	Evans	25 40	74 05	WNW.	12	29.97 m.	37	o. c. g. q.	Clouds NW. and N. Sea H. C. from NW. and WNW.
Ardeo	Clinkard	30 58	73 36	W.	7	29.93 a.	56	c.	Clouds and heavy sea from W. Three hrs. of rainfall.
Aslie	Small	29 23	80 24	NNW.	6	30.05 a.	......	c.	Dry weather. Strong breeze since yesterday noon.
Anna	Menkens	40 48	55 37	ESE.	8	29.77 m.	57	o. g.	High cross sea from NE.
Baltimore	Tremery	41 10	65 40	WSW.	6	29.42 m.	40	c.	Clouds SSW. Sea broken and variable.
Bengore Head	Grady	40 56	59 31	SE.	8	29.22 m.	56	o. r.	Nine a. m. to noon whole gale. Noon shifted to W., heavy rain.
[illegible]*	......	39 02	65 06	WNW.	8	29.55 a.	......	......	......
Brooklyn City	Pitt	40 50	63 51	SW.	12	29.30 a.	41	r.	Strong gale, heavy squalls and rain past day.
Caribbean*	Daniel	35 45	69 10	W. by N.	6	29.56 m.	......	......	At 1 a. m., increasing westerly breeze. Noon, mod. gale and squall.
Catania	Franck	27 00	64 05	N.	4	29.88 a.	69	c. v.	Morning to afternoon, strong gale from SSW., W., NW. Heavy rain. Fine, mod. during night.
City of Chester	Lewis	40 22	61 00	E. & NW.	8	29.32 a.	50	r.	Clouds NW. Cross sea.
City of Lincoln	Fry	34 52	72 27	NNW.	3	29.54	......	c.	Strong, variable wind.
City of San Antonio	Wilder	31 24	80 51	NW.	3	29.95 a.	24	b.	Long swell from SSE.
Colon	Henderson	30 23	72 31	NW.	5	29.97 a.	33	c.	Clear **and fine;** strong breeze; **squally and** heavy sea.
Dora	Meyer	39 56	63 09	NW.	5	29.34 m.	48	o.	Heavy storm, hurricane-like squalls. High, wild sea past day.
Edward E. Barrett*	Hughes	40 25	70 15	SW.	7	29.28 a.		......	Rain and freshening wind and squalls from E. by S. to SSE. At 7 p. m. (C. T.) **hauled** to NW., mod. breeze; **then** heavy W'ly snow squalls to midnight. Barom. slowly rising during the morning.
Elbe	Meyer	43 06	54 32	E.	6	29.82 m.	47	c.	**Strong breezes** and squalls past day.
Fædrelandet	Brunn	37 29	74 57	NW. & SW.	10	29.90 a.	57	g. c.	**Clouds NW.** Heavy sea from N.

* Data obtained by interpolation from journal or storm report. † Storm report gives force of wind 5 all the forenoon.

NOTE.—The City of Lincoln's observation was taken 44 minutes after Greenwich noon.

March 13, 1888.—Continued.

Vessel.	Master.	Position. Lat. N.	Position. Long. W.	Wind. Direction (true).	Wind. Force (Beaufort).	Barometer.	Temp. of air (Fahr.)	Weather by symbols.	Remarks.
France	Hadley	42 31	52 53	E.	4	29.83 a.	54	b. c.	First part clear; fresh NE. winds. Latter mod., E'ly winds.
Glenborn*	Johansen	33 20	60 42	W. by S.	8	29.78 m.			From fine weather to cloudy, squally and W'ly gale. Vivid lightning.
Guido	Ribeyrolle	30 06	70 34	N.	5	30.10 a.	......	b.	Mod. sea from N.
Larne	Fox	42 13	51 40	E.	2	29.55 m.	50	c.	Mod. to fresh breezes.
Julius	Vieira	28 38	78 32	NNW.	6	30.01 a.	61	b. c.	Clouds NNW.; sea N.; air clear.
Kansas	Greig	43 37	36 50	ENE.	5	29.88 m.	45	o. m.	Clouds NE. Sea smooth.
Kennett	Smith	39 15	72 56	WNW.	8	29.32 a.	24	s.	High sea from W. and N. Continuous snow past day.
Knickerbocker	Kemble	27 00	74 35	NW.	4	29.71 m.	77	c.	Clear weather. Heavy puffs throughout the day.
Lake Superior	Stewart	42 58	37 11	E.	6	29.80 m.	41	b.	Strong winds all day.
Lampasas	Crowell	29 55	80 28	N.	4	30.17 a.	55	b.	Fine weather; fresh gale from NNE. past day.
La Normandie	de Kersabiec	41 29	54 01	E.	7	29.93 m.	......	c. g.	Clouds and heavy sea from E.
Lida Fowler*	Higgins	34 00	73 10	W.	9	29.41 a.			Heavy SE. gale shifting formerly to a SW. hurricane, with snow and hail at noon (72d); then hauling to W. and moderating.
Lord Clive	Urquhart	39 46	73 20	WNW.	11	29.41 m.	16	o. s. q.	Tremendous, confused sea and heavy snow squalls.
Lord Gough	Hughes	38 33	57 01	E.	2	29.82 m.	37	c.	Mod. and cloudy weather past day.
Lorenzo D. Baker	Wiley	36 15	73 47	NW.	5	30.04 a.	64	c.	Good weather past day.
Lucy W. Snow	Burgess	36 06	35 22	S.	7	29.79 a.	70	c. q.	Clouds W. Cross sea WSW.
Lydian Monarch	Haggett	40 35	66 14	SW.	11	28.49 m.	34	s.	First part, heavy SE. gale; latter part, heavy SW. gale.
Manhattan	Stevens	25 06	80 35	NNW.	5	30.11 a.	70	b.	Clouds NW. and N. Sea C., ENE.
Nantucket	Richardson	37 00	71 50	NNW.	10	29.56 a.		g. b. r. s.	Bad weather; terrible cross seas from NW. and NNE.
Nessmore	Elliott	39 44	60 29	NW.	6	29.37 m.	41	c. o.	NE'ly gale and squally. Very high sea past day.
New Orleans	Rainey	34 18	66 21	NW.	6	30.12 a.	56	b.	Fine and clear. Heavy to fresh NW. gale past day.
Newport	Shackford	38 53	75 41	W.	11	29.81 a.	30	o. c. q.	Clouds W. Heavy NW'ly sea.
Orinoco	Garvin	32 22	64 46	W.	6	29.84 a.	58	b. c.	Fine weather past day.
Oxford	Jones	41 05	53 42	ENE.	7	29.34 a.		c.	Clouds S. and ESE. Rough broken sea, ENE. and ESE.
Richmond Hill	Hyde	42 31	60 45	SW.	5	29.39 m.	31	s. q.	Strong gale to fresh breezes, with little snow squalls.
Rugia	Karlowa	41 51	50 32	NE. by E.	5	29.86 m.	35	f. c.	Clouds and rough ENE'ly sea.
Samana	Dornquist	33 40	74 40	NW.	10	29.84 a.		o. s.	Clouds NW. Sea G. E. from NNW.
Serapis*	Dobson	39 43	72 40	NW.	12	29.27 a.		......	Thick snow and hurricane from NW. all day.
Slavonia	Schmidt	45 15	33 20	E.	5	29.44 m.	44	b.	Fine weather past day.
State of Georgia	Moodie	41 05	58 28	SW.	7	29.33 a.	34	s.	Wind unsteady and var. between S. and W. Snow showers.
State of Texas	Williams	28 30	74 46	NW.	11	29.88 a.	......	q. s.	Rough NNW. sea.
Stockholm City	Thompson	42 31	56 12	E.	4	29.43 a.	34	c.	Violent SE'ly gale. Terrific snow squalls past day.
St. Ronans	Campbell	41 05	56 46	SE.	4	29.30 a.	34	c. o.	Variable gloomy weather past day.
Switzerland	Ickeneng	38 00	66 36	WSW.	7	29.54 a.	38	c. s.	Increasing to strong SE. gale shifting to WSW. at 11.45.
The Queen	Hewer	40 27	58 36	SW.	6	29.29 a.	30	c. q. s.	Clouds SW. Sea S. from WSW.
Wakefield*	Crowell	35 15	66 15	NW.	6	30.03 a.	....	....	
Wandrahm	Rohe	44 35	67 45	E.	9	29.21 a.	......	r. s. h.	Strong gale all night with much rain, snow, and hail.

March 13, 1888—Continued.

Vessel.	Master.	Position.		Wind.		Barometer.	Temp. of air (Fahr.).	Weather by symbols.	Remarks.
		Lat. N.	Long. W.	Direction, true.	Force, Beaufort.				
		° ′	° ′				°		
Werra	Bussius	40 10	70 05	WSW.	9	29.34 m.	23	s.	Variable and snowy weather past day.
Westernland	Randle	40 44	59 11	SE. by E.	10	29.29 m.	57	o. q.	Mod. to whole gale; thick weather; rain squalls past day.

March 14, 1888.

Vessel.	Master.	Lat. N.	Long. W.	Direction, true.	Force, Beaufort.	Barometer.	Temp. of air (Fahr.).	Weather by symbols.	Remarks.
Ailsa	Evans	37 07	74 00	NW.	10	29.63 m.	35	o. g. u. s.	High cross sea. Heavy sleet.
Alamo	Risk	25 06	80 15	NNW.	7	30.04 a.	......	b. q.	Very fine, puffy. Wind backing to W'd.
Andes	Klinkael	26 48	74 30	W.	8	29.87 a.	67	c.	High sea from West.
Anna	Meckline	41 16	54 58	W. by N.	4	29.47 m.	57	r.	2 p. m., 13th, to mid., whole gale from E.; then heavy rain squalls.
Anita	Small	29 34	75 25	NW.	10	29.60 a.	......	......	NW. gale all the past day.
Baltimore	Traacey	33 43	69 47	NE.	3	29.64 m.	37	c.	Clouds from W. Sea, South and cross.
Bengore Head	Brady	42 00	58 40	WSW.	6	29.33 m.	55	b.	Wind died away at 1 p. m., and was var. all night. Old sea E'ly.
Benison*	Aitkenhead	30 00	65 00	N.	8	29.50 a.	......	......	Fresh gale backing from NW. to W.
Brooklyn City	Fitt	41 28	52 33	WSW.	4	29.45 a.	50	b. c.	Clouds SW. Var. winds. Very confused sea.
Caribbean*	Daniel	31 05	56 05	WSW.	4	29.55 m.	......	......	Occasional rain, cross sea from NE. and SSW.
Celtic	Irving	44 11	49 57	E. by N.	4	29.88 m.	47	b. c. m.	Increasing breeze. Mod. ENE. sea.
City of Chester	Lewis	40 04	55 50	NNW.	5	29.52 a.	53	c.	Clouds from NW. Cross sea from ESE.
City of Lincoln†	Fry	32 32	60 20	SW.	5	29.64 m.	......	o. c.	Strong var. winds and rain past day.
Colon	Henderson	26 30	74 58	WNW.	5	30.02 a.	66	b.	Fine weather. Mod. NW. sea.
Dora	Meyer	39 56	60 34	SW. by W.	5	29.50 m.	52	o. q. r.	Light variable winds. Squally air past day.
Faedrelandet	Bruun	35 00	74 41	NW. by N.	9	29.80 a.	46	o. u.	Whole gale. Heavy lightning during night. Passing fall of snow.
France	Hadley	41 30	57 22	WSW.	5	29.49 a.	48	b.	1st part fr. to mod. E'ly gale; then heavy rain, wind veering to WSW., ending fresh breeze and clear.
Folda	Ringk	41 35	66 13	WNW.	4-5	30.15 m.	30	b.	Mod. WNW. sea.
Glenburn*	Johansen	34 30	61 36	SW. by S.	4	29.88 m.	......	......	1st part clear, W'ly winds. 2d part p. g. l. Last part clearing; SW'ly wind.
Guido	Echeverria	29 30	77 30	NW. by W.	7	29.94 a.	......	b. c.	Past day strong breeze; heavy sea. Squalls every hour.
Julius	Vieira	29 36	77 15	NW.	7	29.93 a.	65	c.	Clouds and broken sea from NW. Air very clear.
Kansas	Gleig	42 23	64 34	NE.	4	29.62 m.	34	m.	Clouds from NE. **Sea smooth.**
Kennett	Smith	39 10	72 00	E.	5	29.41 a.	30	c.	Rough NW. **sea. Snow** all night.
Knickerbocker	Kemble	40 10	73 50	N.	8	29.50 m.	24	o. c.	Gloomy, with frequent snow squalls; boisterous thro'out.
Lake Superior	Stewart	43 49	50 26	E. by N.	6	29.61 m.	40	c.	Strong winds thro'out the day.
Lampasas	Crowell	23 35	77 55	NW. by W.	7	29.89 a.	47	b.	Fresh gale from NNW., backing to NW. by W.
Lida Fowler*	Higgins	38 00	70 15	NW. by N.	3	29.80 a.	......	......	NW. gale, with snow, **mod.** during the night to a gentle NNW. breeze. Bar. rising.
Lord Clive	**Urquhart**	**38 58**	74 10	NW.	**9**	29.77 m.	**18**	**s. q.**	Heavy snow squalls.
Lucy W. Snow	**Durgee**	**30 40**	55 29	WSW.	**3**	29.95 a.	**67**	**b. c.**	**Fair weather. Long NW.** swell.

* Data obtained by interpolation from journal **or storm report.**

† The City of Lincoln's observation was **taken 1 hour and 20 minutes after Greenwich, noon.**

March 14, 1888—Continued.

Vessel.	Master.	Position. Lat. N.	Position. Long. W.	Wind. Direction, true.	Wind. Force, Beaufort.	Barometer.	Temp. of air (Fahr.).	Weather by symbols.	Remarks.
Lydian Monarch	Haggett	40 51	72 45	NE.	3	29.78 m.	37	s.	Clouds from NE. Rough SW. sea.
Nantucket	Richardson	37 16	70 50	N.	8	29.63 a.	......	g. h. r. s.	Very bad weather. Heavy cross seas.
Nederland	Griffin	41 05	49 53	E.	6	29.65 m.	42	r.	Lt. to fr. E. wind, clear; long NE. swell past day.
Newmore	Elliott	36 47	59 24	SW.	6	29.50 m.	61	v. h. c.	Variable winds. High cross sea past day.
Newport	Shackford	42 13	73 58	NNE.	7	29.66 a.	32	c. s.	Rough NW. sea. Thick with snow.
Orinoco	Garvin	32 22	64 50	W.	4	29.90 a.	54	c.	Clouds W. and NW. Past day showery and squally.
Oxford	James	41 20	51 29	ESE.	5	29.58 a.	......	o.	Strong gale, heavy sea. Much rain past day.
Polaria	Schade	36 57	75 40	NW.	5	29.87 a.	37	o. q.	Clouds and mod. sea NW.
Richmond Hill	Hyde	45 10	62 50	E. by N.	3	29.53 m.	42	b. c.	Long NE. sea; squally with showers.
Samana	Hasenpohl	33 45	75 00	NW.	9	29.72 a.	......	o. g.	High cross sea. W. and NW. gale past day.
Slavonia	Schmidt	42 09	51 20	NNE.	5	29.45 m.	46	o.	Long NE. sea. Stormy weather past day.
State of Georgia	Moodie	44 27	71 33	E. by N.	4	29.60 a.	31	o. q.	Clouds NNE. Sea smooth.
Stockholm City	Thompson	42 38	63 27	NE.	3	29.90 a.	39	o. m. s.	Mod. wind; fog from 12 hrs. to 22 hrs., then cleared; fr. breeze.
St. Romans	Campbell	40 47	62 46	N.	7	29.50 m.	55	b.	Long NE. sea. Past day gloomy with rain and lightning.
Switzerland	Ueberweg	38 37	59 29	W.	2	29.70 a.	31	b. v.	Wind decreasing gradually; passing lt. snow showers past day.
New Orleans	Halsey	25 56	80 02	W.	3	30.15 a.	60	b.	Smooth sea; clear and fine past day.
Wandrahm	Rohse	44 36	60 41	NE.	6	29.72 a.	......	o. q.	Mod. NE. sea.
Westernland	Randle	40 42	54 27	W.	4	29.50 m.	60	b. c.	Whole gale 1st part. Wind hauled to W., with mod. breeze.
Wakefield*	Crowell	37 00	65 58	W. by N.	9	29.87 a.	......	......	Wind and sea increasing. At 8 p.m. heavy wind and rain squall from NNW.

* Data obtained by interpolation from journal or storm report.

INDEX TO NAMES OF VESSELS.

The following is a complete list of vessels mentioned in this report, with references to the page or pages where each is mentioned. Although not all of these vessels encountered the storm, some names appearing only incidentally in the text, yet a very large majority of them did, and all the data at hand from each one of them can be readily referred to by means of this index:

www.ingramcontent.com/pod-product-compliance
Lightning Source LLC
Chambersburg PA
CBHW020338090426
42735CB00009B/1588
9783337187002